OUR ACCEPTED SINS

By

Keith Black

ISBN 978-1-959172-69-7

Black Management Publishing

Flower Mound, Texas

Table of Contents

Foreword

"You might need a little humor before you dive into this book."

- Billy Baker, AKA - The Most Humble Book Promoter

What?!

You actually purchased this book?

What were you thinking?

Are you kidding me - do you love to beat yourself up?

This is a book about sinners and you already know very well that is what you are!

Oh, man!

Very well, now that you've bought it, I guess you should just read it and see what happens.

Can I tell you a secret? The author, Keith Black might be some kind of a sick man who likes to see other people feel miserable.

OK, OK, I am going to go out on a limb and say that maybe, it is possible, although I doubt it, that you bought this book for self-improvement.

Well, if that is true, sorry partner, you will have to face some of the "Accepted Sins" in your life.

I hope you don't cry like a baby and just quit reading the chapters in this book. Even if some of the chapters don't apply to you (yeah right) then at least you might use some thoughts to help your weaker brother or sister. God knows there are plenty of those people around.

Sincerely,

Billy Baker, Promotor Par Excellence and weird friend of the author, Keith Black

About This Book

This book, *"Our Accepted Sins"* is for any Christian who wants to live the abundant life in Christ by challenging themselves to eliminate their accepted sins. The author has produced a practical self-help guide to help believers in their daily walk as they battle pride, worldly superstitions, a lack of self-control, greed, and many other sins that rob us from having a fuller relationship with God. This book is a tool for anyone who wants to apply Biblical counsel, but may have failed to take action steps toward a victorious lifestyle.

Daniel C. shared,

> *"I wanted a deeper relationship with God, but something was holding me back (accepted sin). I am happy to have discovered this book. I plan on keeping and referencing it all my life. I am also purchasing copies for my teenage children."*

Gerry T. said,

> *"This book enlightened and challenged me to be introspective. I want everyone in my family to have their own copy."*

Kim T. shared,

> *"Every Chapter spoke to me, thanks for the insight."*

Introduction

The Apostle Paul said,

"I do not understand what I do. For what I want to do, I do not do, but what I hate, I do."

(Romans 7:15 NIV)

Paul admitted here that he was a sinner and even labeled himself, "Chief of Sinners." Paul does not blame anyone for his sins, he accepts full responsibility.

Believers today are no different than Paul. Despite our relationship with God through Christ we are sinners for sure; and although we don't want to sin, nonetheless we do so often that perhaps we have learned to adopt some sins as a regular lifestyle pattern.

"If we say that we have no sin, we are deceiving ourselves, and the truth is not in us."

(I John 1:8 NIV)

Some sins may have become *"Our Accepted Sins"*. We all want to know the truth and especially the truth about sin. The problem is we live in a world where there is so much untruth. We live in a world where truth-tellers are oftentimes, attacked, and sometimes Christians are confused by all the noise and debate.

We often contemplate, what is sin? There is a tremendous spiritual battle in an effort to define exactly what sinful activity is and what is not. Obviously, the first requirement to know sin is to know where to get the truth.

In my younger years, I would watch television and movies that involved courtroom dramas where the witness would walk up to the Judge's bench just prior to delivering their testimony. The witness would raise their right hand while placing their left hand on a Bible and repeat this statement. "I promise to tell the truth, I promise to tell the whole truth, I promise to tell nothing but the truth, so help me God." Otherwise, the Judge may have expressed this as a question to the witness by saying, "Do you solemnly promise to tell the truth, the whole truth, and nothing but the truth? If so, say, I do."

Sadly, this same pledge is rarely required for a witness in today's courtrooms. As judges and the courtroom jury continued their challenge to be the arbiters of truth during trials, they were not convinced that the oath they utilized to swear in witnesses was useful. Polygraph tests were developed, which were supposed to determine if a person was lying or telling the truth. After many years of use in the courtroom, this test was eliminated for one good reason. The polygraph did not work very well! It turned out a machine that simply recorded blood pressure fluctuations was not a good measure of truth telling. Use of the polygraph test was abandoned in most courts beginning around 1998 when rulings and judgements repeatedly stated that the jury or judge, once again, are to be the arbiters of truth.

Every Christian today is just like that man or woman on the witness stand. The question posed to Christian witnesses is how will we live our lives? Will we speak and live the truth about sin, or sadly, will we ignore sin in our lives? Will we call sin for what it is, or will we adopt a worldly standard that calls sin by another name?

The good news is every Christian has a guidebook provided by God. We should pattern our lives after the teachings in God's Word. The Bible is the Christian's arbiter of truth.

Now, if we proclaim the Bible is the living Word of God, then we must accept it as truth. So, if the Bible says that an action, or a thought is a sin, then it is a sin. To put it another way, and I am certainly not trying to be even a little delicate here when I say that, "Your personal opinion about sin really does not matter at all!"

To worldly influencers, the Bible is just an antiquated book of fiction based on ideas that, in their opinion, promotes hate speech. To the secularist, the idea that one would quote or reference the Bible is an affront in itself. We live in a time when wise Christians are being silenced and canceled so that ignorant people won't be offended.

In contrast, the Christian understands that God, who is the powerful creator of the universe and all good things, has provided His Holy Scriptures for our guidance and edification. Who would literally be so foolish than to debate God? Well, sadly, there are many that would indeed be so foolish.

We cannot get a full picture of sin and its effects without looking at our Lord. We know God hates sin, and He has said,

"He would by no means clear the guilty."

(Exodus 34:7 KJV)

As we look closely at the life and actions of our Lord and Savior, Jesus Christ, we first must understand, he was completely without sin. Jesus lived his life as a kind, compassionate spiritual leader, teaching and offering forgiveness of sins to whosoever would humble themselves by admitting their sin and come to a saving knowledge of Christ. Only Jesus, the sinless, Son of God could be worthy to give us salvation by willingly taking our sins upon himself.

Prior to our salvation decision, our sin fully separated us from God. Once we have prayed to receive Christ, suddenly we are literally transformed. See Romans 12:2. Our mindset toward sin is changed. After becoming a Christian, we should want to please God and pattern our life after Christ.

This book is designed to help Christians target sins that God wants us to eliminate. Bible verses are provided to help the reader better understand how God wants us to live. God wants us to be victorious and take full ownership, and if we do, He promises an abundant life, filled with joy as we serve Him here on earth.

Although this book could serve as an individual study guide for personal edification, the author has also designed it to be useful in small groups. Christians may come together as they review the book to grow spiritually and encourage one another in their Christian walk.

First, read the Scriptures in each of the 15 sin-related topics and reflect on the questions. Prayerfully ask God to help you see if there is any sin He wants you to address, or otherwise discern how you can encourage and lift up your brothers and sisters in Christ.

Chapter 1: Pride, Boasting and a Self-Centered Lifestyle

Everyone has things they like, and also things they do not like. I like warm sunny days, cheeseburgers, action movies, sports, and a round of golf. I do not like spinach, kale, broccoli, dancing, and liars.

Ever wonder what God likes? Well, we know He loves us so much he sent His Son to the Cross. He loves us to worship Him. He delights for us to serve Him and have a meek disposition. He wants us to have both joy and peace and He has graciously provided many blessings and promises as we walk the Christian life.

God also has provided clear insight as to what He does not like. In fact, He makes it clear that there are some things He hates. Yes, and just so there is no doubt, He has provided a list. Proverbs lists the things the Lord hates.

Let's look at what the Bible says.

"There are six things the Lord hates, seven that are detestable to Him; haughty eyes, a lying tongue, hands that shed innocent blood, a heart that devises wicked schemes, feet that are quick to rush into evil, a false witness who pours out lies, and a person who stirs up conflict in the community."

(Proverbs 6:16-19NIV)

What is the number one sin on the list of things the Lord hates? What does it mean to have "haughty eyes"? In Proverbs 21, haughty eyes are mentioned again and linked to a proud heart. The King James Version simply identifies this as a, "proud look".

I love the Contemporary English Version here. The verse says,

"Evil people are proud and arrogant, but sin is the only crop they produce."

(Proverbs 21:4 CEV)

To have an arrogant disposition or demeanor is to foster an evil lifestyle of scorning, or looking down on others while thinking like an elitist.

If you think you are just a better person, you are not! It is true some may have been blessed with attractiveness, a fine mind, wealth, or athleticism, but does that really make anyone better in God's eyes. This is an affront to God the Creator because He formed us. He gifted us. Did God bless anyone so they could look down on the rest of His Creation? Did God choose anyone to devalue His Creation?

This lesson points out Biblical perspectives, which will enlighten us on how to effectively defeat our tendency to fall into a prideful state when we engage in boasting along with a self-centered lifestyle.

Ask yourself, what causes today's person to be inclined to exhibit these ungodly characteristics?

_____

_____

_____

_____

First, let's review some additional verses and see what they have to say about how God feels about pride.

Read:

"God opposes the proud but shows favor to the humble."

(James 4:6 NIV)

"He mocks proud mockers but shows favor to the humble and oppressed."

(Proverbs 3:34 NIV)

"See I am against you, you arrogant one, declares the Lord, the Lord Almighty, for your day has come, the time for you to be punished."

(Jeremiah 50:31, 32 NIV)

"For everything in the world-the lust of the flesh, the lust of the eyes, and the pride of life-is not from the Father but is from the world."

14

(I John 2:16 NIV)

"The proud look of man will be abased, and the loftiness of man will be humbled, and the Lord alone will be exalted in the day." "I will punish the world for its evil, the wicked for their sins. I will put an end to the arrogance of the haughty and will humble the pride of the ruthless."

(Isaiah 2:11, 12 and 13:11 NIV)

"We have heard the pride of Moab-he is very proud-of his haughtiness, his pride, his arrogance and his self-exaltation. The terror you inspire and the pride of your heart has deceived you, you who live in the clefts of the rocks, who occupy the heights of the hill. Though you build your nest as high as the eagle's, from there I will bring you down, declares the Lord."

(Jeremiah 48:29, 30 and 49:16 NIV)

What do these verses say is inevitably going to happen to the me generation and those who are consumed with pride?

_____

_____

_____

_____

List some Biblical characters who engaged in prideful boasting and were cast down. How about listing some modern-day examples?

_____

_____

_____

_____

The Pharisees loved to praise one another and Jesus called them out on this in John's book.

"How can you believe since you accept glory from one another but do not seek the glory that comes from the only God?"

(John 5:44 NIV)

It is not uncommon for proud, arrogant people to try to build one another up. We know personal pride is the number one reason why Christ is rejected by the unbelieving world. We understand that in order to become a Christian we must first humble ourselves while admitting our sin and our hopeless state of being.

Despite this, many Christians still fall victim to the sin of pride. After reading God's word, and clearly understanding God's hatred of pride, we need to be asking ourselves how we can overcome pride in our lives.

God not only condemns pride, but He offers wise counsel on how to defeat pride in our walk.

Read:

"In the same way, you who are younger, submit yourselves to your elders. All of you, clothe yourselves with humility toward one another, because, God opposes the proud but shows favor to the humble. Humble yourselves, therefore, under God's mighty hand, that He may lift you up in due time."

(I Peter 5:5, 6 NIV)

"But they (Joseph and Mary) did not understand the statement which He had made to them. And when He went down with them and came to Nazareth, and He continued in subjection to them; and His mother treasured all these things in her heart. And Jesus kept increasing in wisdom and stature, and in favor with God and men."

(Luke 2:50-52 NIV)

"Do not speak against one another, brethren. He who speaks against a brother or judges his brother, speaks against the law and judges the law, you are not a doer of the law but a judge of it. There is only one Lawgiver and Judge, the One who is able to save and to destroy; but who are you who judge your neighbor. Come now, you who say, today or tomorrow we will go to such and such a city, and spend a year there and engage in business and make a profit. Yet you do not know what your life will be like tomorrow. You are just a vapor that appears for a little while and then vanishes away. Instead, you ought to say, if the Lord wills, we will do this or that. But as it is, you boast in your arrogance: all such boasting is evil. Therefore to one who knows the right thing to do and does not do it, to him it is sin."

(James 4:11-17 NIV)

"When pride comes, then comes disgrace, but with humility comes wisdom."

(Proverbs 11:2 NIV)

"Love is patient, love is kind and not jealous: love does not brag and is not arrogant, does not act unbecomingly: it does not seek its own, is not provoked, does not take into account a wrong suffered."

(I Corinthians 13:4, 5NIV)

How does the Bible say we can overcome the sins of pride and arrogance?

_____

_____

_____

_____

For an unbeliever, failing to repent the sins in their life, results in a rejection of God leading to eternal damnation. For a Christian, to choose not to claim the victory over prideful sin is a choice to limit fellowship with God affecting all other aspects of life. We can deal with pride and maintain legitimate self-esteem.

To get started here are some practical ideas:

- Ask God to help you overcome any pride in your life.
- Listen, listen, and listen, when others are talking. Don't interrupt,
- Make it a point not to tell everybody about your accomplishments.
- Understand that God may have given you a special talent or a fine intellect. Thank God for this, and be kind to those who possess talents different from yours.
- Understand you are not indispensable.
- Find ways to serve others and do it.
- Give an anonymous gift or help a stranger without recognition or reward.
- Find out the needs of others and pray for them.

Chapter 2: A Lack of Self-Control Regarding Health Matters

This chapter addresses biblical perspectives on today's degradation in the Christians lack of self-control or self-discipline regarding health matters such as getting proper rest, exercising, and eating healthy.

I Corinthians says,

"Do you not know that your bodies are temples of the Holy Spirit, who is in you, whom you have received from God? You are not your own; you were bought at a price. Therefore honor God with your bodies."

(I Corinthians 6:19-20 NIV)

How would you rate yourself on getting proper rest, exercise, and eating right? On a range of one to ten, with one representing poor self-discipline, and ten, representing excellent self-discipline, where are you?

Today we are privileged to have access to a great amount of information on how poor health habits may harm our bodies. Well, that is good to have, but the Bible has a lot to say about this topic? We love to read the story from I Kings Chapter 18, where Elijah called fire down from heaven and defeated the prophets of Baal.

Read Elijah's prayer.

"Lord..., let it be known that you are God in Israel and that I am your servant and have done all of these things at your command."

(I Kings 18: 35 NIV)

Elijah had won a great victory and even taunted his enemies, and as if that was not enough, he ran on foot from Mt. Carmel to Jezreel. That is 25 miles, almost a marathon! Even more impressive is the fact that Elijah literally out ran the King's Chariot.

I have run a couple of marathons, and I can tell you from personal experience that after completing them, my state of being was hungry and tired. Imagine how Elijah felt at this time.

Then, in the very next Chapter, I Kings 19, we see a great contrast where this same Elijah runs away with great fear. He hides in a cave, and asks God to take his own life.

What is happening here? How could a servant of God be so bold and strong one day, and then, be so discouraged, fearful, and weak the next day? Is this the same man?

Well, that is exactly what God asked.

"What are you doing here Elijah?"

(I Kings 19:6 NIV)

There are multiple reasons for Elijah's spiritual failure and discouragement, but it is interesting to see what the Lord does to reinvigorate him. The Lord sends His angel to minister to Elijah.

Let's read about it.

"He lay down and slept under a juniper tree; and behold, there was an angel touching him, and he said to him, "Arise, eat." Then he looked and behold, there was at his head a bread cake baked on hot stones, and a jar of water. So he ate and drank and lay down again."

(I Kings 19:5-9 NIV)

Later Elijah falsely claims he is the only faithful follower in the fight against the evil Baal worshipers. God responds and encourages Elijah by pointing out that there are actually 7,000 more faithful followers in the fight against Baal.

After the great victory on Mt. Carmel, what do you think are some of the reasons for Elijah's negative transformation and discouragement?

_____

_____

_____

_____

Specifically, what did God have His angel do for Elijah to strengthen and reinvigorate his faith?

_____

_____

_____

_____

Do you agree that a lack of sleep or hunger can change a person and even affect our faith? Yes or no? Why is this so?

_____

_____

_____

_____

In your opinion, with so many modern conveniences available today, why do so many complain of tiredness?

_____

_____

_____

_____

Now that I have encouraged you to get the proper amount of rest and keep yourself fully nourished, allow me to move on to another health matter, gluttony.

Read the following verses:

"Listen my son, and be wise, And direct your heart in the way. Do not be with heavy drinkers of wine, Or with glutinous eaters of meat; For the heavy drinker and the glutton will come to poverty, And drowsiness will clothe one with rags."

(Proverbs 23:19-21) NIV

"A discerning son heeds instruction, but a companion of gluttons disgraces his father."

(Proverbs 28:7 NIV)

"These wicked people are heavy and prosperous; their waists bulge with fat."

(Job 15:27 NIV)

Merriam Webster's Collegiate Dictionary: Tenth Edition defines a glutton as, "One habitually given to greedy and voracious eating and drinking."

Gluttony, simply put, is a lack of self-discipline and a rejection of reasonable behavior. Self-control is a fruit of the Holy Spirit, and without it, we cannot be successful as Christians. It is foundational to win the victory over sin. Clearly, gluttony is a lack of self-control.

Medical officials assert that the number of overweight and obese people in the USA is more than ever before in history. We are regularly warned about the negative health effects of obesity. The obesity rate is estimated to be more than four in every ten adult people worldwide. "The National Center for Health Statistics at the CDC revealed in their most recent data that over 42% of U.S. adults are obese. Obesity is defined as an adult man or woman with a body mass index (BMI) of 30 or higher." (1)

Why does God condemn gluttony so strongly? Why does God care if we are overweight?

_____
_____
_____
_____

Finally, ask yourself these questions.

- Do I overeat?
- Am I getting enough sleep?

- Do I practice enough self-discipline in my eating habits and my sleep schedule?

- Am I often too tired to have meaningful quiet times with God?

- Do I exercise regularly?

- Do I make excuses for my overeating or tiredness?

- Will I commit to making changes in my life?

- What specific goals will you seek to achieve?

- Will you commit these issues to prayer and ask God to help you as you seek to change?

Here are some practical ideas to help you get started on your quest to practice self-control in these areas:

- Seek counsel from your doctor on health-related matters.

- Set up a regular schedule that allows you to get enough sleep.

- Try not to be on your computer or other electronic devices prior to bedtime.

- Try to eat better foods avoiding unhealthy snacks and fast foods.

- With professional medical expert opinions, determine the best weight for yourself and take measures to reduce your weight if necessary. If you exceed you weight goal include both exercise and proper eating habits to address the overweight condition. It is best to regularly maintain these habits- bingeing is proven to be counter-productive.

- Purchase a scale to keep track of your ongoing efforts.

- Tell a Christian friend and prayer partner about your decision to get your weight under control.

- Understand that weight control is a lifetime commitment.

Chapter 3: Worldly Superstitions and Evil Spirits

Superstitions and evil spirits permeate our society. Christians must be on guard so these worldly practices and influences do not creep into our lives. Superstition is defined as an irrational belief in the supernatural where luck or magic has the power to change a life. The Bible does not support the idea that things happen by chance. Therefore, superstition evolves from ignorance or out of some fear of the unknown; it could even be an overt, conscious effort to seek some kind of spirit counsel apart from God.

Evil spirits are referenced in both the Old and New Testaments and otherwise are sometimes called demons, unclean spirits or impure spirits. Evil Spirits know exactly who Jesus is and that they face future condemnation and judgement.

"What do you want from us, Son of God?" they shouted. "Have you come here to torture us before the appointed time?"

(Matthew 8:29 NIV)

Jesus dealt with another evil spirit named Legion in the Gospel of Mark.

"He shouted at the top of his voice, "What do you want with me, Jesus, Son of the Most High God? In God's name don't torture me!" For Jesus had said to him, "Come out of this man, you impure spirit!"

(Mark 5:7, 8 NIV)

We may innocently begin our day by reading the local newspaper where each edition is sure not to forget to include the horoscope section. It is hard to understand why anyone would have any connection or involvement in horoscopes. Why anyone would choose to worship the creation, when they could, otherwise, worship the Almighty Creator. As we progress through our day we may watch television, or be online where we are solicited to make a contact with a physic.

Often, we experience superstitions more subtly. Perhaps we enter a building where the 13th floor is not listed on the elevator. No doubt you experience this on a personal level when someone wishes you "good luck". We hear people say, knock on wood, or don't break a mirror, walk under a ladder, or step on a crack. How do these simple sayings cause the weaker believer to lose their focus on God?

We may also be exposed to an advertisement for a palm reader, astrologer, or tarot card interpreter. In fact, while doing some online research for this very topic, I received several pop-up advertisements asking if I wanted to consult with a medium. No thanks! After reading King Saul's scriptural epitaph in Chronicles, that is the last thing I would ever want to participate in, or be a party to.

The verses say,

"Saul died because he was unfaithful to the Lord.... And even consulted a medium for guidance and did not inquire of the Lord, so the Lord put him to death."

NIV (Chronicles 10:13, 14)

Today unbelievers will bring up the word, "karma", while espousing their idea of the principle of sowing and reaping. They falsely imply that getting good or bad future outcomes (in the present or afterlife) is based on personal works. Consider that an open invitation to share how, "God's word says we are all sinners." Furthermore, pointing out, "It's only through believing in the saving power of Jesus Christ that anyone could have a better afterlife." This statement usually ends the discussion about karma. You might want to take that same approach.

If someone were to ask if you would be open to engaging in any sort of occult like activity, please know this, evil spirits are dangerous because they involve deceit and lies and may even involve contact with evil, fallen angels. Christians <u>must</u> avoid involvement in this sinful behavior. Still, Satan effectively utilizes this as a tool to keep an unbeliever from thinking clearly about Jesus Christ.

"...among whom the god of this system (Satan)of things has blinded the minds of the unbelievers, so that the illumination of the glorious good news about the Christ, who is the image of God, might not shine through."

(2 Corinthians 4:4 NIV)

Our Lord has demonstrated a different standard for us and a complete intolerance for these ungodly practices.

Read:

"When you enter the land of the Lord your God is giving you, do not learn to imitate the detestable ways of the nations there. Let no one be found among you who sacrifices their son or daughter in the fire, who practices divination or sorcery, interprets omens, engages in witchcraft, or casts spells, or who is a medium or spiritist or who consults the dead. Anyone who does these things is detestable to the Lord: because of these same detestable practices the Lord your God will drive out those nations before you. You must be blameless before the Lord your God. The nations you will repossess listen to those who practice sorcery or divination. But as for you, the Lord your God has not permitted you to do so."

(Deuteronomy 18:9-14 NIV)

Why do you think God has so strongly condemned superstitious and evil spiritual activities?

_____

_____

_____

Have you ever participated in superstition, the occult, or evil spiritual activities? How did you feel about your participation afterward? What would you do differently today?

_____
_____
_____
_____

Do you think the activities mentioned above can be a form of idolatry? Why or why not?

_____
_____
_____
_____

One of the most idolatrous and superstitious people of all time were the Greeks who lived in Athens during the time of the Apostle Paul. They had an idol for everything and just in case they inadvertently missed one, they even made a statute to the, "unknown god". We read in Acts,

"For as I walked around and looked carefully at your objects of worship, I even found an altar with this inscription: TO AN UNKNOWN GOD. So you are ignorant of the very thing you worship - and this is what I am going to proclaim to you."

(Acts 17:23 NIV)

Paul effectively appeals to their culture to gain their attention and an opening to present the Gospel. What innovative ways can you use the existence of contemporary idolatry or superstition to gain an opportunity to witness?

_____
_____
_____
_____

The Bible gives us guidance on how to protect ourselves from these evil influences in James.

"Therefore subject yourselves to God; but oppose the Devil, and he will flee from you. Draw close to God, and He will draw close to you. Cleanse your hands, you sinners, and purify your hearts, you indecisive ones."

(James 4:7, 8 NIV)

Practical points to ponder:

- When we give credence to superstitions, we deny God's will.

- Our God has demonstrated through His Word that a conscious involvement in the occult or dark spirits is deemed to be a grievous sin, with consequences often leading to death and destruction.

Here are some ideas to get you started on your quest to practice self-control in eliminating worldly superstitions:

- Focus on your speech as best you can, to eliminate certain words that deny God such as lucky, karma, horoscope, chance, etc.

- Purpose in your heart to never dabble in the occult or dark spirits and educate your children about the devastating risks and effects.

- If your spirit is troubled when watching, listening, or reading, then immediately separate yourself from that influence.

- Eliminate anything in your home and environment that could desensitize you to evil things, which might open a link to superstition, the occult or dark spirits.

- Pray and ask God to place a hedge of protection around you and your family.

Chapter 4: Failure to Spend Time in God's World

Someone once said we would hardly change at all if not for the books we read or the people we meet. Do you know the title of the number one best seller for all books this year? What about last year and the year before that? It is the Bible! The Bible is the most translated book in history. Over five billion copies of the Bible have been sold.

There is no other book like the Bible. The world's number one bestseller every year is truly inspired by our Lord. God has a great desire to communicate with us. Consider that God led 40 authors over a period of 1600 years to write His inspiring message, the living Word of God. If we are to change for good, if we are to understand God's will for our lives, if we are to be what God wants us to be, then we simply must read His word regularly.

There are many competing interests to keep us from spending even a little time reading the Bible. We allow online social media and popular websites to steal our time. Imagine if all the time on these sites was spent reading the Bible. A nice thought but not reality.

Do you have a desire to read the Bible consistently? Why or Why not?

_____

_____

_____

_____

If you feel you have time constraints that are keeping you from God's Word, consider your priorities and look at some online programs where you can listen to someone else read scripture. You could easily do this while driving. I downloaded the YouVersion Bible on my cellphone, and I read it every day. When I enter the site each morning, I see a message that says, "Good Morning, Keith." They show me my daily streak for site visits. They have devotional plans and challenges to read through the Bible with podcasts, videos, and all kinds of resources. I would encourage everyone to do this because it is so easy. If I could get you to just do this, at the minimum, for even one minute each day, I would take that. Come on, what's your excuse? I know you can do it now!

Let's look at a few verses in Scripture on this topic:

"For the word of God is alive, and active, sharper than any double-edged sword, it penetrates even to dividing soul and spirit, joints and marrow, it judges the thoughts and attitudes of the heart."

(Hebrews 4:12 NIV)

The Bible teaches us about sin. As you read it, you will be convicted of your sin, and you will learn how to overcome them.

"Do your best to present yourself to God as one approved, a worker who does not need to be ashamed and who correctly handles the word of truth.

(II Timothy 2:15 NIV)

You will learn how God wants you to live and act as a believer.

"All Scripture is God-breathed and is useful for teaching, rebuking, correcting and training in righteousness, so that the servant of God may be thoroughly equipped for every good work."

(II Timothy 3:16 NIV)

You will be trained on how to serve God.

"Blessed is the one who reads aloud the words of this prophecy, and blessed are those who hear it and take to heart what is written in it, because the time is near.

(Revelation 1:3 NIV)

You will have knowledge for today and hope for the future.

"I consider that our present sufferings are not worth comparing with the glory that will be revealed in us."

(Romans 8:18 NIV)

Here are some practical ideas to help you get started on your plan to spend more time in God's word:

- Download a popular free online Bible APP onto your cellphone. Three suggestions include YouVersion Bible, Bible Gateway, or BibleHub.

- Set a goal to read the Bible every day. Try at least 15 minutes, but even 5 is better than nothing. You can do this!

- Advance by reading more and set goals to read Books of the Bible, memorize verses, and join a Bible study through your Church.

- If you are new to Bible reading, you may want to choose the New International Version (NIV), and then start by reading the Gospel of John in the New Testament. Then read the book of Acts.

- The Bible teaches that we need brothers and sisters in the faith for inspiration and support. Ask a friend to join you in a Bible reading accountability challenge.

- The Bible is known as the Living Word of God because it changes lives, and it will change you. Certainly, you will be blessed by spending time in God's Word.

- Pray and ask God to bless your efforts, ask Him to help you to keep your commitment to read His Word, and to help you interpret His Scriptures.

A consistent reading of God's Word comes with tremendous benefits and incentives. These can include:

1. Wisdom and Knowledge

2. Peace and Joy

3. Discernment and Insight in Decision Making

4. Power to Fight Against the Devil and Worldly Influences

Chapter 5: Failure to Claim Our God-Given Possessions

In Numbers Chapter 13, the Israelites received their report from the spies concerning the inhabitants of the promised land. Unfortunately, they accepted the majority report, rejecting the minority report from Joshua and Caleb. Although they still were the children of God, an entire generation wasted their lives by not having faith and choosing not to possess their God-given possession, the promised land. No doubt, some Israelites chose to live in fear instead of trusting God, and some simply did not want to take on the hard challenge of fighting for the land God had given to them. Either way, this was a lack of faith. The Israelites missed out on many of God's blessings. God did not abandon them, but their poor personal choice resulted in their lives being more difficult.

Are there any possessions that God has offered to you that you have chosen not to possess? Do you feel this may have caused you to miss out on some blessings?

_____

_____

_____

_____

_____

In this Chapter, we will focus on four potential areas where God expects us to step up and take ownership. In each area, there is much at stake. If you choose not to master these areas in your life, then you will be in the wilderness, missing out on some of God's blessings.

1. Taking A Leadership Role In Your Home

When we say that God challenges us to be a spiritual leader at home, exactly who is God challenging to do this? Read Ephesians 22-33 and note there is counsel here to both husbands and wives. These verses are certainly not just for men only. Proverbs Chapter 31 also specifically addresses the role of wives in the home. In order to be a spiritual leader in the home, you need to have a strong relationship with God. Different leadership roles do not mean inferiority in any way.

Dr. James Dobson has said,

"Most well-functioning Christian homes with both husbands and wives make decisions together as equals."

Both two-parent and single parents should serve as "servant leaders" with love while leading all family members to follow God. We have a clear picture of the results of a failure to lead in this area by looking at Biblical figures, including King David's dysfunctional family.

Have you accepted your role as a spiritual leader in your home? What are the implications of a yes or no response?

_____
_____
_____
_____
_____

2. Utilizing Your Spiritual Gifts

Every Christian needs to know and understand what their spiritual gifts are. The Body of Christ (the Church) cannot function as well as it should unless all members are active in exercising their gifts. God made you a unique individual, and you were given certain gifts by God. Read I Corinthians 12:8-10, 28, and I Peter 4:8-11. Most spiritual gift models identify at least 20 or more gift areas. These gifts are given to be used, not to be unutilized. Read I Corinthians 12:12-14.

Are you utilizing your spiritual gifts? What are the implications of a yes or no response?

_____
_____
_____
_____
_____

3. Pray

Every Christian has a responsibility to pray. God tells us to pray without ceasing! For this lesson, we will focus our attention on just two verses in the book of James, which talk about why a Christian may fail at praying.

"You do not have because you do not ask God. When you ask, you do not receive, because you ask with wrong motives, that you may spend what you get on your pleasures."

(James 4:2-3 NIV)

This scripture teaches us that we need to pray regularly. Some feel-good pastors today stop there and misstate the main reason for unanswered prayer. Prayer is not designed to fulfill our needs and wants. God really does want to bless our prayers but simply put, our prayers need to focus on helping others and glorifying God, not ourselves.

Do you have the power of prayer in your life? What are the implications of a yes or no response?

_____

_____

_____

_____

Finally, Read Ephesians 6:18.

"And pray in the Spirit on all occasions with all kinds of prayers and requests. With this in mind, be alert and always keep on praying for all the Lord's people."

(Ephesians 6:18 *NIV*)

4. Tithe

In Malachi, God makes it very clear that we have a choice to make, and we can choose either a curse or a blessing. The verses say,

"Will a mere mortal rob God? Yet you rob me. But you ask, How are we robbing you? In tithes and offerings. You are under a curse your whole nation-because you are robbing me. Bring the whole tithe into the storehouse, that there may be food in my house. Test me in this, says the Lord Almighty, and see if I will not throw open the floodgates of heaven and pour out so much blessing that there will not be room enough to store it."

(Malachi 3:8-11 NIV)

Do you give your tithes and offerings to the Lord? What are the implications of a yes or no response?

_____

_____

_____

_____

Can you think of other God-given possessions that we often fail to possess?

_____

_____

_____

_____

Read how we can fully trust in God's promises.

"So the Lord gave Israel all the land he had sworn to give their ancestors, and they took possession of it and settled there. The Lord gave them rest on every side, just as he had sworn to their ancestors. Not one of their enemies withstood them; the Lord gave all their enemies into their hands. Not one of all the Lord's good promises to Israel failed; every one was fulfilled."

(Joshua 21:43-45 NIV)

Chapter 6: Failure to Fight the Good Fight

Jesus espoused meekness, but not weakness, and His life here on earth proved this. Jesus was outspoken, and He was not politically correct in the face of the greatest evil opposition in the history of the world. While focusing on the Gospel message, He also delved into discussions of all things sin. This included divorce, sexual promiscuity, and the love of money, pride, lying, and anything else, which causes people to be separated from God. Jesus also challenged the religious elitist Pharisees and called them liars and vipers. He literally whipped the moneychangers out of the Temple and spoke the truth in God's Synagogues, despite vocal enemies. Jesus also knew very well there remained an ongoing plot to kill Him.

What if, just like Jesus, you are mocked, criticized, spat upon, threatened, plotted against, threatened, falsely accused, arrested without merit, deceived, and even abandoned by those who are supposed to love and support you? No person can say exactly how much opposition you may receive as you share your faith, but for sure, we do know some worldly opposition is going to come. Your reaction to worldly opposition is your story.

Just prior to his martyrdom in 67AD, Paul wrote in II Timothy,

"I have fought the good fight, I have finished the race, I have kept the faith."

(II Timothy 4:7 NIV)

Paul was saying that he had an unwavering faith and love for the Gospel of Jesus Christ. No matter what suffering or hardships he faced, Paul was undeterred from his ministry. Paul was an ever-vigilant warrior for the faith. There was no quitting despite the challenges of hardship, stoning, prison, or poverty. Like Jesus, he called sin for what it is and did not allow his enemies to influence his positions or speech.

So two obvious questions to ask ourselves at this time are: What does "fighting the good fight" mean for us today? And what might keep us from fighting the good fight? First, "fighting the good fight" means that we consider Christ's sacrifice as our greatest gift. As Christians, we are to live a life worthy of our calling. Of course, we do not earn our salvation, but we rather serve Christ out of love and gratitude for what He has done. Paul tells Timothy exactly how to live a life of service in Christ.

"But you, man of God, flee from all this, and pursue righteousness, godliness, faith, love, endurance and gentleness. Fight the good fight of the faith. Take hold of the eternal life to which you were called when you made your good confession in the presence of many witnesses."

(I Timothy 6: 11-12 NIV)

I doubt anyone said it better than the late Charles Colson in his famous book titled, How Now Shall We Live. Colson discusses how today's "Christian needs to first have an understanding of God's Word, which will give them the confidence and the tools to confront the world's bankrupt worldviews and to restore and redeem every aspect of contemporary culture. This includes family, education, ethics, work, law, politics, science, art, and music."

Secondly, there are many excuses that may keep believers from fighting the good fight. Included among these are fear, complacency, love of this world, addiction to sin, or ingratitude. Maybe Christians have also failed to prepare for the fight.

"Put on full armor of God so that you can take your stand against the devils schemes."

(Ephesians 6:11 NIV)

46

Earlier in II Timothy 6:12, we read where Paul tells believers to think long term. Our lives are eternal, so we should live our lives with this in mind. As Paul was near his death here on earth, he mentioned the *"Crown of Righteousness."* Paul looks forward to receiving this reward in Heaven. This is not a crown based on works but on Jesus's work for us. Focusing on Christ's return at the rapture will help us to fight the good fight.

Do you feel that you can say at this time that you have fought the good fight? If not, what changes could you make at this time?

_____

_____

_____

_____

After I received Christ as my personal Savior as a 9-year-old, I wanted to share my faith with others. I often witnessed this to my young neighborhood playmates and later to my teenage peers. Some of my neighborhood buddies would go to church with me, and some prayed to receive Christ.

Later on, when I was about 18 years of age, I had a very memorable event happen in my life. This one particular day, I was getting a haircut from a gentleman who I am guessing was approximately 60 years old. I was at a barbershop across town. As the barber cut my hair, I decided to share my faith with him. Of course, I did not know how the barber would react, particularly with me being a lot younger than him. I remember being pleased that the barber listened patiently and quietly.

When he had finished cutting my hair, I thanked him and paid him, and then he finally spoke. What he said to me stunned me, and I have never forgotten his words. He looked straight at me and said, *"Young man, your faith is full now while you are young, but when you are older like me, you will forsake your religion."* I was raised to respect my elders, so I just thanked him for letting me share my faith. Then, as I walked out of the barbershop, I just stood there outside of the shop door, and I felt compelled to bow my head and pray. I do not remember the exact words of my prayer, but I do know that right there on that sidewalk, I asked God never to let that man's prophecy come true. In my prayer, I told God that I was purposing in my heart to honor and serve Him for all of my life, and I asked God to give me the strength of faith and perseverance to honor my commitment.

Someday we will all stand before God. There is one thing we all want to hear our Lord say, "Well done thou good and faithful servant."

"Blessed is the one who perseveres under trial because, having stood the test, that person will receive the crown of life that the Lord has promised to those who love Him."

(James 1:12 NIV)

If you feel you are lacking at all in keeping the faith and fighting the good fight, here are some things you should do:

1) Read and study God's Word regularly. The Bible says,

"How can a young person stay on the path of purity? By living according to your word. I have hidden your word in my heart that I might not sin against you."

(Psalms 119:9, 11 NIV)

2) Understand that following God's word is your demonstration of love and faith toward God.

"If you love me, keep my commands."

(John 14:15 NIV)

3) As you pray, ask God to help you to develop a long-term perspective as you live in your temporary home here on earth.

"For we know that if our earthly tent we live in is destroyed, we have a building from God, an eternal house in heaven, not built by human hands."

(II Corinthians 5:1 NIV)

4) Purpose in your heart to boldly share your faith with others.

"For I am not ashamed of the gospel, because it is the power of God that brings salvation to everyone who believes..."

(Romans 1: 16 NIV)

5) Understand that God has given you a secret weapon in your struggle to fight the good fight. When you are weak, God's Holy Spirit will strengthen you. When you are tempted, the Holy Spirit will convict you, and when you need help, the Holy Spirit will intercede for you. Read Romans Chapter 8 verse 11,

"... he who raised Christ from the dead is living in you, he who raised Christ from the dead will also give life to your mortal bodies because of his Spirit who lives in you."

In the same way, the Spirit helps us in our prayers. Even when you cannot find the right words to pray, the Spirit will be there to help you.

"We do not know what we ought to pray for, but the Spirit himself intercedes for us...."

(Romans 8:11 NIV)

6) Finally, ask God to show you areas of ministry according to your spiritual gifts and get involved in service. Make I Corinthians 15:58 a prominent verse in your life.

"Therefore, my dear brothers and sisters, stand firm. Let nothing move you. Always give yourselves fully to the work of the Lord, because you know that your labor in the Lord is not in vain."

(I Corinthians 15:58 NIV)

Chapter 7: Preoccupation with Recreational Activities

We are all given the same amount of time to use at our discretion. Do you ever give a second thought to how you use your time when you are not working, or is this something you rarely think about? What does the Bible say? Let's look at this verse.

"Woe to those who rise early in the morning to run after their drinks, who stay up late at night till they are inflamed with wine. They have harps and lyres at their banquets, pipes and trembles and wine, but they have no regard for the deeds of the Lord, no respect for the work of His hands."

(Isaiah 5: 11-12 NIV)

We should establish the fact that leisure time is in no way sinful. Hiking, fishing, camping, organized sports, travel/vacationing, aerobics, and numerous other activities are all perfectly acceptable with benefits to both our health and mental fitness. It is God who even set aside one day each week for rest. See Exodus 20:8-11. Music, dance, festivals, and feasts are all endorsed in scripture. So we conclude that recreational activities are acceptable, except when they displace our Godly focus.

Those referred to in the verse above were solely focused on their own pleasureful interests from sun-up to sundown. They seemed to have no time to respect the work of the Lord or fellowship with Him. Seems like Isaiah is describing a lot of people who constantly pursue a life of leisure and alcoholism while forgetting about God. How relevant and sad that this verse is so applicable in today's world.

Do you think the verse in Isaiah only applies to unbelievers? Think again! A recent New York Times article stated that a Gallup survey revealed that 73% of Americans attended church regularly in 1937, but today that number has fallen below 50%. The percentage of church attendance has dropped most significantly among younger parents and children. Ever wonder what those who have abandoned church attendance are doing with their time?

As an older grandparent, I can say with experience that youth sports on Sundays were generally unavailable prior to this last decade or two. Today, however, with the emergence of more sports teams designed for participants with lower skill sets all the way up to elite levels, youth sports programs have emerged to consume huge amounts of family time. It is not unusual for youth sports teams to have at least one weekly practice along with tournament games on weekends. These tournaments can span from sun-up to sundown on both Saturdays and Sundays. Some tournaments are even hundreds of miles away for children who are ten or older. Whether it is the pursuit of a scholarship or even just the love of the sport, too many Christian parents are failing in their duty to: dedicate time to worship the Lord, spend time studying His word, and fellowshipping with other believers. Every day their children internalize this terrible example from their parent's actions.

Perhaps the best way to judge whether or not we may have a problem in this area is to just use one of God's commands as a measure.

"And let us consider how we may spur one another on toward love and good deeds, not giving up meeting together, as some are in the habit of doing, but encouraging one another — and all the more as you see the Day approaching."

(Hebrews 10: 24-25, NIV)

Just as an athlete needs to prepare to run the race, believers today need to consistently recharge their spiritual batteries. This verse, however, points out more than just the simple need for regular church attendance. Christians are to encourage one another. We often forget that part of Hebrews 10:25. Remember, God says it is not all about you. We are to pray for one another. We are to build up, exhort, and teach one another. Yes, you need to hear the word regularly to be strong in the Lord, but God also points out that you have a job to do, and that job is not watching your child swing a bat or kick a soccer ball at the time when you should be in a public worship service.

Here is some Godly counsel for our youth.

"You who are young, be happy while you are young, and let your heart give you joy in the days of your youth. Follow the ways of your heart and whatever your eyes see, but know that for all these things God will bring you into judgement."

(Ecclesiastes 11: 9 NIV)

To me, this verse is saying, your life is a gift from God. Enjoy your youth! However, young people, you must understand that God will hold you accountable. Both regular and ongoing exposure to God's word is imperative for our youth to be properly equipped to stand upright in this sinful world. Take your children to church and get them involved in Christian youth activities and serving others.

In your own words, what is the Biblical view of recreational activities?

_____

_____

_____

_____

On average, how much time do you spend watching television, online programs, movies, or recreational activities? How does your response compare with the time you spend in God's word, praying or ministering to others?

_____

_____

_____

_____

" Our days may come to seventy years, or eighty, if our strength endures: yet the best of them are but trouble and sorrow, for they quickly pass, and we fly away. Teach us to number our days, that we may gain a heart of wisdom.

(Psalms 90:10, 12 NIV)

"Be very careful, then, how you live — not as unwise but as wise, making the most of every opportunity, because the days are evil. Therefore do not be foolish, but understand what the Lord's will is."

(Ephesians 5:15-17 NIV)

"Do you not know that in a race all the runners run, but only one gets the prize? Run in such a way as to get the prize. Therefore I do not run like someone running aimlessly; I do not fight like a boxer beating the air. No, I strike a blow to my body and make it my slave so that after I have preached to others, I myself will not be disqualified for the prize."

(I Corinthians 9:24, 26-27 NIV)

"For physical training is of some value, but godliness has value for all things, holding promise for both the present life and the life to come."

(I Timothy 4:7 NIV)

Points to Ponder

Reflecting on these verses, how can we use our time more in keeping with the Biblical mandate?

_____
_____
_____
_____

On your own, read Luke 12:19-21 and Matthew 25:14-30. Although Jesus' main point in these verses is not to condemn recreational activity, why do you think Jesus so frequently used examples that condemn recreational/non-productive activity?

_____

_____

_____

_____

I accepted Christ as my Savior as a 9-year-old 4th Grader while attending Calvary Baptist Church in Covington, Kentucky. My Pastor was named Warren Wiersbe. Our Church had a great youth program that helped me to grow spiritually, and I loved studying God's word. My new Christian friends were awesome.

Near the same time in my life, during the early 60s, I became active in the Boy Scouts. I loved hiking, camping, cooking on an open fire, and sleeping in tents. What fun! I also had some great friendships with members of my Local Scout Troop, Number 766. I invited a few Scouts to my Church. I rose in rank as a Scout and took on leadership roles like Patrol Leader and Junior Assistant Scoutmaster. Sometimes our Troop would go on full weekend campouts.

This caused a dilemma for me. I was not comfortable missing Church during those weekend campouts. After discussing this with my parents and my Scoutmaster, I decided to go to weekend campouts, which sometimes began on Friday evenings. I would stay with the Troop through Saturday evening and then go home so I could attend my Church on Sunday morning. I was the only kid that did this, so it was kind of isolating, but I knew it was the right thing to do. Now, I am not saying that I had any significant influence on this, but later our Scoutmaster, Mr. Guy King, became a Christian himself.

Sometimes Christians have to take a stand, and at other times, they just need to separate themselves. I knew this because Warren Wiersbe wrote a book that I read. The title was "Romans - How to Be Right with God, Yourself, and Others. I remember Pastor Wiersbe referring to Romans as "The Letter to the Non-Conformist." In his book, he shared how sometimes believers just need to be different, set apart from the world.

"Do not conform to the pattern of this world, but be transformed by the renewing of your mind. Then you will be able to test and approve what God's will is—His good, pleasing and perfect will."

(Romans 12:2 NIV)

Sometimes even the simplest of decisions can have a lifelong impact.

Action items:

- Go to Church and take your family!

- Listen to the sermon. Worship God!

- Give to the ministry and serve!

- Pray, Honor God, and love others!

Chapter 8: Slavery to Lust/Greed

When a friend saw this Chapter title, he asked, "Why address the sins of lust and greed in the same chapter?" The answer is that the words, lust and greed, have similar meanings. Greed is a synonym for lust. As a noun, we define lust as a feeling of strong desire, often of a sexual nature, although one could lust after other things like food as well. Greed may be defined simply as lust expressed in nonsexual ways. Another way to define greed is to say that it is an intense desire to want more than is needed or required. Targets for greed are often money/riches, possessions, power, or fame.

While writing this book, admittedly, I wondered if God would choose to bless my efforts. One way many authors would measure this is to look at book sales. Knowing very little about the publishing world, I discovered there are some predatory publishers that are called "vanity press" publishers. They will charge authors high fees to publish their books at levels well above their actual expenses and normal profit expectations. These publishers do not really care if the book sells or not cause they capture up-front fees. They make money doing this because authors or writers are often so in love with their writings that they will agree to pay a vanity press publisher just to see their name on a book. To say it another way, some authors are vain. So whether it is out of the author's personal vanity, ignorance or greed, financially speaking, these vanity press publishers seem to earn generous profits.

These examples point to the fact that the world knows and understands lust and greed for what it is, and numerous business models are created every day to prey on this sinful weakness.

In like manner, an investor can make a few dollars in the stock market. Following this, due to their own pride and greed, some may take more risks than they should. We know this oftentimes results in disastrous consequences. When Christians think about gambling, the word "greed" usually comes to mind. There is a reason that Las Vegas casinos thrive! When your State Lottery Board promotes their version of the "Jackpot," they focus their message on what you may possibly receive as the winner because they know appealing to your greed will more likely cause you to act to buy a lottery ticket. You will never hear lottery commercials boldly pointing out how many people have to lose in order that one person may win. Stating this kind of reality is not their business model.

Perhaps the ultimate lust is the desire among people to be their own God in this world. Pride, lust, and greed are intertwined in our sinful nature.

Here is what the Bible says,

"Do not love the world or anything in the world. If anyone loves the world, love for the Father is not in them. For everything in the world—the lust of the flesh, the lust of the eyes, and the pride of life—comes not from the Father but from the world."

(I John 2:15, 16 NIV)

What role do you think comparing your situation to someone else plays in the "wanting more" process? It has been said, "comparison is inevitable." What does that say about the state of mankind?

_____

_____

_____

_____

Read these verses related to lust/greed and answer the questions below.

"But each person is tempted when they are dragged away by their own evil desire and enticed. Then after desire has conceived, it gives birth to sin; and sin, when it is full grown gives way to death."

(James 1:14, 15 NIV)

"You desire but do not have, so you kill. You covet but you cannot get what you want, so you quarrel and fight. You do not have because you do not ask God."

(James 2:2, 3 NIV)

"But the worries of this life, the deceitfulness of wealth and the desires for other things come in and choke the word, making it unfruitful.

(Mark 4:19 NIV)

"Those who want to get rich fall into temptation and a trap and into many foolish and harmful desires that plunge people into ruin and destruction. For the love of money is a root of all kinds of evil. Some people, eager for money, have wondered from the faith and pierced themselves with many griefs."

(I Timothy 6:9, 10 NIV)

What are some of the results of wanting more? Will lust/greed get in the way of our relationship and service to God?

_____

_____

_____

_____

Read these verses and answer the questions below.

"Keep you lives free from the love of money and be content with what you have, because God has said, Never will I leave you; never will I forsake you."

(Hebrews 13: 5 NIV)

"Those who belong to Jesus Christ have crucified the flesh with its passions and desires. Since we live by the Spirit, let us keep in step with the Spirit. Let us not become conceited, provoking and envying each other."

(Galatians 5:24-26 NIV)

"Then he said to them, 'Watch out! Be on your guard against all kinds of greed; life does not consist in an abundance of possessions. And he told them this parable: 'The ground of a certain rich man yielded an abundant harvest. He thought to himself, "What shall I do? I have no place to store my crops." Then he said, "This is what I'll do. I will tear down my barns and build bigger ones, and there I will store my surplus grain. And I'll say to myself, 'You have plenty of grain laid up for many years. Take life easy; eat, drink and be merry.' "But God said to him, "You fool! This very night your life will be demanded from you. Then who will get what you have prepared for yourself?" This is how it will be with whoever stores up things for themselves but is not rich towards God. Then Jesus said to his disciples: 'Therefore I tell you, do not worry about your life, what you will eat; or about your body, what you will wear. For life is more than food, and the body more than clothes. Consider the ravens: they do not sow or reap, they have no storeroom or barn; yet God feeds them. And how much more valuable you are than birds!"

(Luke 12:15-24 NIV)

If lust/greed is a part of our nature, how can it be conquered?

_____

_____

_____

_____

Today in the USA, what criterion do we use to distinguish between wants and needs? What should our attitude be toward our needs? Our wants?

_____

_____

_____

_____

If you feel you are lacking at all in defeating lust/greed, here are some things you should try.

First, you must ask God in prayer to help change you.

Ask God to renew your mind and help you to think about how to live your life with eternal considerations. Quit thinking about the things on this earth and how you plan on amassing great wealth. You know you can't take any possessions with you!

"Then he said to them, watch out! Be on guard against all kinds of greed; life does not consist in an abundance of possessions."

(Luke 12:15 NIV)

Start honoring God by helping the poor and less fortunate.

"Whoever oppresses the poor shows contempt for their Maker, but whoever is kind to the needy honors God."

(Proverbs 14:31 NIV)

Being content with the Lord is a learned process. I'll address this topic more fully in Chapter 9, but for now, **stop loving money and be content with what the Lord has provided to you**. Claim the Lord's promises and free yourself from worry.

"Never will I leave you, never will I forsake you."

(Hebrews 13:5 NIV)

"The greedy stir up conflict, but those who trust in the Lord will prosper."

(Proverbs 28:25 NIV)

Give to the Lord!

"The generous will themselves be blessed, for they share their food with the poor."

(Proverbs 22:9 NIV)

"The stingy are eager to get rich and are unaware that poverty awaits them."

(Proverbs 28:22 NIV)

Some people spend their entire life obsessing over the accumulation of wealth. Even if they reach their goals, they will just set new, higher ones. If the Lord truly is our shepherd, then we shall not want. How many times have we repeated the very beginning of the famous Psalm without internalizing these words?

"The Lord is my shepherd, I shall not want…"

(Psalm 23:1 KJV)

Chapter 9: A Lack of Contentment

Shakespeare's famous play, "Richard III," is filled with murder and deceit. The main character, "Richard III," utters this famous line at the opening, "Now is the Winter of our Discontent...." The world apart from God will never be satisfied and will suffer from chronic discontent.

The me generation wants more. It is all about riches, power, or fame. We understand how the world's model to measure success ultimately results in discontent. It's the psychiatrist full employment act! If anyone believes that they may be content by obtaining enough worldly possessions, then that person will forever be subject to a life of discontent. How do I know they are shooting at the wrong target? God's Word, of course. – Read:

"He who trusts in his riches will fall, But the righteous will flourish like the green leaf."

(Proverbs 11:28 NIV)

"For the love of money is a root of all sorts of evil. Some people, eager for money, have wandered away from the faith and pierced themselves with many griefs."

(I Timothy 6:10 NIV)

Sadly today, even believers experience a lack of contentment. We just talked about lust and greed, and we concluded that without contentment, these sins flourish, but conversely, with contentment, we win victory over many sins. If contentment were a gift from God, then a joyous, abundant life would be easier to attain. If this were true, fear, worry, lust, and greed might just fade away.

Scripture makes it clear that contentment is not a gift. It must be learned and sought after by every believer. Paul states this truth.

"Not that I speak in respect of want: for I have learned, in whatsoever state I am, therewith to be content."

(Philippians 4:11 KJV)

We strive to face the challenges of the Christian life and to pattern our lives after Jesus Christ. Just like in Paul's life, God may allow suffering, disappointment, poverty, sickness, and even persecution to come into our lives. Paul tells us more about this.

"I know what it is to be in need, and I know what it is to have plenty. I have learned the secret of being content in any and every situation, whether well fed or hungry, whether living in plenty or in want."

(Philippians 4:12 NIV)

"Listen my dear brothers and sisters: Has not God chosen those who are poor in the eyes of the world to be rich in faith and to inherit the kingdom he promised those who love him?"

(James 2:5 NIV)

Think about the fruits of the Spirit. Love, joy, peace, kindness, etc. The fruits of the Spirit should be growing within all believers. These fruits can only grow, however, when we humbly seek to serve our Lord. We prepare our hearts while seeking God's will, just like the farmer prepares his soil to grow crops. Some farmers are better at this, and some Christians are more content than others.

"But seek first his kingdom and his righteousness, and all these things will be given to you as well."

(Matthew 6:33 NIV)

The secret to being content may be in the definition itself, not only what the true meaning of contentment is, but also what it is not. Real Godly contentment is freedom from being controlled by the worldly definition of contentment.

Some may ask, is it OK for believers to have financial goals, plan for retirement, or think about purchases? Of course, as Christians, we are challenged to manage those assets that God has entrusted to us. You must manage money, and you are free to enjoy the fruits of your labor. As an MBA, I feel gifted by our Lord, in particular, to focus on these areas as a ministry. I have taught managing your money using Biblical teachings at churches, in small groups, and in classrooms to both adults and teens. God wants us to effectively manage all assets that he has entrusted to us. Certainly, you can do this and be content because, like the fruits of the Spirit, contentment is a matter of the heart. Remember, God's word says it's the "love of money" that is the root of evil. Money in itself is not evil. It's just a medium of exchange.

Read the verses below and then answer the questions.

"But godliness with contentment is great gain. For we brought nothing into the world, and we can take nothing out of it. But if we have food and clothing, we will be content with that. Those who want to get rich fall into temptation and a trap and into many foolish and harmful desires that plunge people into ruin and destruction."

(I Timothy 6:6-10 NIV)

"Then He said to them, "Watch out!" Be on guard against all kinds of greed; life does not consist of an abundance of possessions."

(Luke 12:15 NIV)

What is your number one area of discontent? Do you often compare yourself to others relative to your income and possessions? Why or Why not?

_____

_____

"Just then a man came to Jesus and asked, "Teacher, what good thing must I do to get eternal life?" Why do you ask me about what is good? Jesus replied. There is only one who is good. If you want to enter life, keep my commandments. Which ones he inquired? Jesus replied, You shall not murder, you shall not commit adultery, you shall not steal, you shall not give false testimony, honor thy father and mother, and love your neighbor as yourself. All these have I kept, the young man said. What do I still lack? Jesus answered, If you want to be perfect, go sell your possessions and give to the poor, and you will have treasure in heaven. Then come, follow me. When the young man heard this he went away sad, because he had great wealth. Then Jesus said to his disciples, Truly I tell you, it is hard for someone who is rich to enter the kingdom of God. When the disciples heard this they were greatly astonished and asked, Who then can be saved? Jesus looked at them and said, With man this is impossible, but with God all things are possible. Peter answered him, We have left everything to follow you! What then will there be for us? Truly I tell you, at the renewal of all things, when the Son of Man sits on his glorious throne, you who have followed me will also sit on twelve thrones, judging the twelve tribes of Israel. And everyone who has left houses or brothers or sisters or father or mother or wife or children or fields for my sake will receive a hundred times as much and will inherit the eternal life. But many who are first will be last, and many who are last will be first.

(Matthew 19:16-30 NIV)

Would you be sad if Jesus commanded you to sell all your possessions to the poor? Yes or No?

Do you think this story of the rich young man is a literal blueprint for how we should conduct our lives as Christians? Yes or No?

Why do you think Jesus instructed the rich young man to sell all his possessions and give to the poor?

_____

_____

_____

_____

How many wealthy Biblical characters can you name who also had great faith? Write their names. Did their wealth hinder their relationship with God? Why or why not?

_____

_____

_____

_____

How did Abraham and Job differ from the rich young man in Matthew 19?

_____

_____

_____

_____

Finish this statement as honestly as you can. I will finally be content when_____

_____

_____

_____

Action items:

- Understand that the path to contentment is hidden from those who are apart from God.

- Remember that the powerful, almighty creator loves you so much that he sent his son to die for you.

- Understand and know that it is God's prerogative to bless you in any manner he sees fit.

- Ask God to forgive you of your discontentment.

- Pray and ask God to help you on your journey to learn to have a thankful heart of contentment.

- Let go of the past and serve God each day while looking forward to our glorious future with the Lord in heaven.

Remember: Contentment turns whatever we have into being enough!

Chapter 10: Failure to Manage Financial Assets God's Way

During my youthful years as a Boy Scout, I reached the rank of First Class scout, but to continue to rise in rank, it was necessary to earn merit badges. Seemed like there were a hundred different options, but the very first merit badge I chose to earn was "personal finances." While in middle school, I would buy penny candy and sell each piece for a nickel out of my locker to earn money. What a fine business I had until one day, the principal shut me down. In High School, my favorite class was General Business, taught by Mr. Massey. God gave me a passion for business even at a young age.

After accepting Christ as my Savior, I was taught that God made me a unique individual. My Church was awesome at helping young believers like me to grow in Bible knowledge. We attended a church camp each year, and a lot of kids would come to a saving knowledge of Christ during that week. On Friday night, we would always have a closing campfire, and anyone could speak and tell how God had blessed them during the week. A few kids said they believed that God was calling them into full-time Christian service, and you know what, many actually did become missionaries all over the world. I remember this one year after the campfire, on the way back to my cabin, my counselor, Bob White, asked me, "Did I feel the Lord's calling for my life." I was not sure how this man would react, but I sheepishly told Him the truth. I said, "I feel like God wants me to be a businessman." It was so encouraging to hear his response. He said, "Well, that is fine, then you should be the best businessman you can be, and you should honor God as a businessman." I was so happy and encouraged that he affirmed what I knew God wanted me to be.

Of course, we know the main theme in scripture is our relationship with God, but because God cares about every aspect of our lives, his book also contains specific guidance and instructions on other topics. There is instruction and insights on health care, hygiene, farming, and many other topics. Seems like God wants us to be successful in every dimension of our lives. Unfortunately, we do not always follow the Godly principles found in his Word.

This chapter presents counsel to help us make better financial decisions. God entrusts assets to our care and management, but there are expectations that should not be ignored. After earning my MBA and reflecting on what I had learned, I concluded decades ago that the Bible is the absolute best business/management text ever written. Let's dive into some powerful messages from God's word. We will attempt to separate this Biblical counsel into two topical areas: Asset Management and Financial Counsel. Before we do that, I want you to look at the list I put together that includes a lot of concerns many believers have today.

What are your most significant financial or financial-related concerns? Place a check wherever you have deep concerns.

_____ Children (care, assistance, support)

_____ Parents (getting older, care)

_____ Job (finding or losing it)

_____ Money (Not having enough)

_____ Advancement (getting ahead)

_____ Transition (starting over)

_____ Mid-life (failing my expectations)

_____ Health (can't afford, the unknown)

_____ Debt (can't pay back)

_____ Retirement (affordability, feeling useless)

_____ Future (being alone)

_____ Other

This is not a list to just gloss over. Pray and ask God to help you address your concerns, and remember, God is able. Sometimes it is wise to talk with Christian counselors about these issues. If you don't know any Christian counselors on the financial side, Dave Ramsay, Ron Blue, and others have some wonderful resources and helpful books. Other organizations like Focus on the Family and so many fine local churches and counselors are there to help. The first two items on our list of concerns are family related. Jesus had tough words for those who evaded their financial responsibilities to their families.

"Anyone who does not provide for their relatives, and especially for their own household, has denied the faith and is worse than an unbeliever."

(I Timothy 5:8 NIV)

Asset Management

Read:

"Do not store up for yourselves treasures on earth, where moths and vermin destroy, and where thieves break in and steal. But store up for yourself treasures in Heaven, where moths and vermin do not destroy, and where thieves do not break in and steal. For where your treasure is there will your heart be also.

(Matthew 6:19-21 NIV)

How should a Christian's value system on assets differ from the world?

_____

_____

_____

_____

Read:

"Again, it will be like a man going on a journey, who called his servants and entrusted his wealth to them. To one he gave five bags of gold, to another two bags, and to another one bag, each according to his ability. Then he went on his journey. The man who received five bags of gold went at once and put his money to work and gained five bags more. So also, the one with two bags of gold gained two more. But the man who had received one bag went off, dug a hole in the ground and hid his master's money. After a long time the master of those servants returned and settled accounts with them. The man who had received five bags of gold brought the other five. Master he said, 'you entrusted me with five bags of gold. See I have gained five more.' "His master replied, 'Well done good and faithful servant! You have been faithful with a few things; I will put you in charge of many things. Come and share your master's happiness!' The man with two bags of gold also came. 'Master he said, 'you entrusted me with two bags of gold; see, I have gained two more.' "His master replied, "Well done, good and faithful servant! You have been faithful with a few things; I will put you in charge of many things. Come and share your master's happiness!" Then the man who had received one bag of gold came. 'Master, he said, 'I knew that you are a hard man, harvesting where you have not sown and gathering where you have not scattered seed. So I was afraid and went out and hid your gold in the ground. See, here is what belongs to you.' His master replied, 'You wicked, lazy servant! So you knew that I harvest where I have not sown and gathered where I have not scattered seed? Well then you should have put my money on deposit with the bankers, so when I returned I would have received it back with interest.' "So take the bag of gold from him and give it to the one who has ten bags. For whoever has, will be given more, and they will have an abundance. Whoever does not have, even what they have will be taken from them. And throw that worthless servant outside, into the darkness, where there will be weeping and gnashing of teeth."

(Matthew 25:14-30 NIV)

Certainly, in these verses, Jesus is encouraging us to be prepared for His Second Coming. Faithful stewardship of time, money and our spiritual gifts are required to be prepared to meet our Master. In the story above, Jesus represents the Master, and Christians are his servants. The gold represents God's gifts that we should be using to serve Christ. The Masters assessment of his servants represents judgement day.

As you acquire assets, do you view them as a means to fulfill God's purposes in your life? Yes or No.

_____

List a few specific examples of how God's financial blessings have helped you to fulfill His purposes in your life.

_____
_____
_____
_____

Financial Counsel

Having taught and led Bible groups on managing money, many Christians have asked me about giving. The word tithe is only found in the Old Testament. I have heard many fine sermons pointing out that there is no other percentage amount mentioned in Scripture except the tithe, meaning ten percent. In the New Testament, there are many verses calling for Christians to give. I like a particular verse in I Corinthians.

"On the first day of the week, each one of you should set aside a sum of money in keeping with your income, saving it up, so that when I come no collections will have to be made."

(I Corinthians 16:2 NIV)

Here we see proportional giving. Therefore percentage giving makes sense. I also see instructions for timely giving on the first day of the week. God's word also instructs we are to give cheerfully and not out of necessity.

The Bible encourages us to limit debt, save, and do budget planning. All this requires self-discipline. I have seen married couples where the man is not the best one to be the money manager and vice versa. When I asked couples the question: who is the best money manager? They always seem to agree and know the answer. That is the one who should manage the family finances.

Read and reflect individually, and if you are using this book as part of a small group, discuss each area of counsel.

1. Discern needs from wants.

"And my God will meet all your needs according to the riches of his glory in Christ Jesus."

(Philippians 4:19 NIV)

2. Realize that God is able to supply funds when a bill is due and discern God's reason for insufficient funds.

"Consider the ravens: They do not sow or reap, they have no storeroom or barn; yet God feeds them. And how much more valuable you are than birds!"

(Luke 12:24 NIV)

3. Use great caution in co-signing for anything.

"My son, if you have put up security for your neighbor, if you have shaken hands in pledge for a stranger, you have been trapped by what you said, ensnared by the words of your mouth."

(Proverbs 6:1, 2 NIV)

Whoever puts up security for a stranger will surely suffer, but whoever refuses to shake hands in pledge is safe."

(Proverbs 11:15)

4. Perform reasonable budget planning and stick to it.

"Suppose one of you wants to build a tower. Won't you first sit down and estimate the cost to see if you have enough money to complete it? For if you lay foundation and are not able to finish it, everyone who sees it will ridicule you, saying, This person began to build and wasn't able to finish."

(Luke 14: 28-30 NIV)

5. A person's ability to give may be determined by what he has already given.

"Remember this: Whoever sows sparingly will also reap sparingly, and whoever sows generously will also reap generously."

(II Corinthians 9:6 NIV)

6. Give to others and tithe with the proper motive.

"Each of you should give what you have decided in your heart to give, not reluctantly or under compulsion, for God loves a cheerful giver."

(II Corinthians 9:7 NIV)

7. Be sure to consult with your spouse when budget planning and before making major purchases to ensure you are both in agreement.

"If a house is divided against itself, that house cannot stand."

(Mark 3:25 NIV)

When managing our money and assets, we, of course, prefer not to learn by the trial and error method. Mistakes can be costly!

What are some mistakes that you have made in managing money or assets? What would you do differently today?

_____

_____

_____

_____

Chapter 11: Thinking Your Sins Are Hidden

There are several instances in scripture where people tried to hide from God. It did not work! When Adam and Eve hid themselves in the Garden, God knew exactly where to find them. When Jonah tried to just sail away, of course, that strategy did not go well for him. Forget about that idea. It failed miserably. These efforts to hide from God seem so ridiculously weak. We ask: what were they thinking? It is a Sin that will cause us to run and attempt to hide from God.

Here is what the Bible says about God.

"Nothing in all creation is hidden from God's sight. Everything is uncovered and laid bare before the eyes of him to whom we must give account."

(Hebrews 4:13 NIV)

The hopeful desire of the author is that this book is to help us engage in reflecting on our accepted sins. It is sad, then, that one of our accepted sins might be that we actually would attempt to hide our sins from God.

"You discern my going out and my lying down; you are familiar with all my ways. Before a word is on my tongue you, Lord, know it completely. You hem me in behind and before, and you lay your hand upon me, too lofty for me to attain. Where can I go from your Spirit?"

(Psalm 139:3-7 NIV)

God was never lost or hidden. It always seemed a little backward for some evangelicals to say, "You need to find God." Anyway, I get their point. The truth is, God our Father is one hundred percent accessible and always will be. He knows everything about us, including where we are, what we are thinking, and what we are doing.

"You have searched me, Lord, and you know me. You know when I sit and when I rise; you perceive my thoughts from afar."

87

Furthermore, God's word says we will give an account of how we live. Just like Adam, we might try to put the blame for our sins on others. Adam's problem was that he was more concerned about the consequences of sin than the sin itself. It appears Adam, the leader, became Adam the follower, much like any believer who allows worldly influences to dictate their actions. Eve also played the blame game.

So what should believers do when we sin? Of course, God's word has the answer.

"If we confess our sins, he is faithful and just and will forgive us our sins and purify us from all unrighteousness."

(I John 1:9 NIV)

Questions Just Between You and God

I have prepared a list of nine questions for you to reflect upon. Please humbly and honestly answer them as an individual. If you are studying this book as part of a small group, I will encourage the group to review these unanswered questions so each group member may answer only to God.

1. Do I act the same way alone as I do when others are watching?

2. Do I treat my spouse/family with love and respect at all times?

3. How often do you seek forgiveness for your sins?

4. Is there anyone you need to forgive?

5. Do you seek acceptance from the world or from God?

6. Do I honor God by investing in eternity?

7. Is there any activity/thing I am doing or involved with that is not honoring God?

8. Do you try to remake God into the image you think he should be?

9. Do I often entertain impure thoughts?

Pray and ask God to help you overcome any area of sin and ask him for forgiveness. Understand and know that God will forgive you! Ask God for strength to overcome any areas of weakness in your Christian walk.

"Whoever conceals their sins does not prosper, but one who confesses and renounces them finds mercy."

(Proverbs 28:13 NIV)

Chapter 12: Poor Decision Making and Making the Right Choices

Of course, we all make decisions each day. Many decisions are not significant, but throughout our lives, there are many decisions to be made that have huge ramifications. Who will we marry, will we go to college or not, and if so, where and what major will we choose? After this, there are employment decisions, real estate purchases, vehicles, family, children's issues, and a myriad of more-to-less important matters to decide upon. Since this book is written to be a guide for believers, we will accept that the most critical life-changing decision, which is to receive Christ and be a part of God's family, has already been made.

I have challenged my grandkids to read one Bible chapter in Proverbs every day while they are young. Like Solomon, of course, I advised that they should ask God for wisdom as they pray. There are so many nuggets of truth in Proverbs. Verse two in Chapter one points out the purpose of the book. *"For obtaining wisdom and self-discipline."* No one can make the best decisions in life without these!

Here are just a few pearls I like to mention that I have paraphrased from Proverbs.

- **Seek after wisdom.** (God would love to grant it to you, and you get it by studying God's Word.) Proverbs 2:6; 3:13-18

- **A soft answer turns away anger.** (Controlling your voice tone and volume reduces tension.) Proverbs 15:1

- **Honor your father and mother**. (God offers a special blessing to those who do this.) Proverbs 6:20-22

- **Accept discipline and constructive criticism**. (This will make you a better person.) Proverbs 10:17

- **In a multitude of counselors, there is safety**. (Ask smart Christians what they might decide on an issue.) Proverbs 11:14

- **Proverbs often identify three kinds of people, and you know which ones to avoid.** Proverbs 1:22; 12:15-20; 9:7-9

    o *Wise* - knows the right thing to do and does it. Proverbs 3:5-7

    o *Fool* - knows the right thing to do but does not do it. Proverbs 18:2; 10:8

    o *Mocker* - makes fun of those who do the right thing. Proverbs 15:2; 22:10; 9:12

- **The fear of the Lord is the beginning of wisdom.** (Those who fear the Lord, hate evil, and love God.) Proverbs 1:7; 9:10

- **A generous man will be blessed.** (Giving to the poor and to the ministry is the same as giving a gift to God.) Proverbs 11:25; 28:27

- **You honor God by working, but the lazy will not prosper.** (You should be known for hard work as unto the Lord.) Proverbs 18:9; 10:4

- **Avoid angry, greedy, ungodly, and mischievous persons.** (They will only cause you trouble.) Proverbs 1:10-19

- **The wise will hear and increase learning.** (You should be quiet and listen, you will learn more.) Proverbs 13:11-13; 19:20; 29:20

- **Let God be your guide and leave judgement to Him** (God is in control, and everyone will face his judgement.) Proverbs 20:22

- **Remain humble** (God hates pride and arrogance.) Proverbs 25:6; 26:12

- **Find Godly friends and hang onto them**. (You will need them, and they will need you) Proverbs 27:10,17

This Proverbial counsel for living and decision-making is to be used for all of our lives.

"The believer's mind ought to be so saturated with divine truth that it can determine the divine perspective on decisions that must be made. A renewed mind is alert to the world's false philosophies and Satan's subtle strategy." (2)

- Warren Wiersbe

Here is what this quote from Warren Wiersbe is saying, "if you really know your Bible, you will make better decisions." That's the first key part. The second part of his quote says, "Your mind needs to be renewed." I stated this in an earlier chapter, but it needs to be repeated. A renewed mind is a mind that is transformed with a desire and passion for honoring God.

"Do not conform to the pattern of this world, but be ye transformed by the renewing of your mind."

(Romans 12:2 NIV)

Here is another quote in my Bible from a Warren Wiersbe sermon from way back in 1970. His words were, "It is OK to mark in your Bible, but make sure that your Bible marks you!" (3). I was fortunate that he was my Pastor. I loved him for teaching and training me in the truth.

A lack of attention to biblical teaching in decision-making will result in bad decisions. Check with any Christian counselor today, and they will tell you they are busy helping others to find peace and a better path forward due to the results of poor decisions. A careful study of the life of King David reveals how his terrible decisions resulted in turmoil and a lifetime of regret for himself. Unfortunately, his sins, including lust for the flesh, failure to lead, and a lack of training in self-discipline, further illustrate how bad decisions can affect an entire family network. We know God is faithful and just to forgive our sins, but the results of sin can tear our lives to shreds.

A careful review and study of the "Principles for Practical Decision Making" (listed below) points out that, as Christians, we have three dimensions of responsibility in decision-making. Someone shared these thoughts with me over fifty years ago. I have unsuccessfully searched high and low to figure out where it came from, so I can properly credit and cite it as a reference. Someone said it looked like a Navigators illustration, but I have yet to prove that is where this originated. Anyway, I want my readers to know that **I did not originate these principles, but I have been blessed to have them**, and I am happy to share this with you because they are timeless truths.

If you are in a group study, please complete your Bible Study today by reading each line and having someone read each verse. If you are reading this book on your own, I will challenge you to do the same.

Principles for Practical Decision Making

Responsibility to Oneself

A. Don't be brought under the power of anything. (Allow nothing to become habit forming but God and his will) – I Corinthians 6:12

B. Avoid things that don't help you grow. – I Corinthians 10:23

C. Avoid doubtful things. If in doubt, don't. – Romans 14:22, 23 and I Thessalonians 5:22

D. Don't waste time. – Ephesians 5:16

E. Our bodies are the temple of the Holy Spirit: Don't defile them. – I Corinthians 6:19, 20: 3:16

Responsibility to Others

1st - Family (I Timothy 5:8); 2nd - Other Believers (Galatians 6:10); 3rd - Everyone Else (Romans 15:1, 2).

A. Don't be a stumbling block. – Romans 14:13, 21 and I Corinthians 8:9

B. Seek for the good and edification of others. – Romans 14:19; 15:1, 2 and I Corinthians 10: 23, 24

Responsibility to God

A. We belong to Jesus, and we should live like it. – Romans 14:8 and I Corinthians 6:20

B. Do all things for God's glory. – I Corinthians 10:31

C. We will all give an account to God. – Romans 14:12

"A Christian must not merely consider what is lawful, but what is expedient, and to edify others."(4)

-   **Matthew Henry**

Do you give your spouse or otherwise believers the freedom to offer counsel regarding important decisions in your life? Yes or No?

_____

When making important decisions, do you ever ask yourself, what does the Bible have to say on this matter? Yes or No?

_____

Think of a few examples where worldly counsel and godly counsel are completely diverse. List a few and contrast the differences. Such as the worldly view and the Godly view on sin, money, relationships, and personal goals.

_____
_____
_____
_____
_____

Read:

"Do not be yoked together with unbelievers. For what do righteousness and wickedness have in common? Or what fellowship can light have with darkness?"

(I Corinthians 6:14 NIV)

To what circumstances does this verse apply? Can you list any Biblical characters that best illustrate the devastating effects of not following this counsel?

_____

_____

_____

_____

Making the Right Choice

How did Daniel successfully face moral and ethical challenges? Read from the book of Daniel:

"But Daniel resolved not to defile himself with the royal food and wine, and he asked the chief official for permission not to defile himself this way. Now God had caused the official to show favor and compassion to Daniel, but the official told Daniel, 'I am afraid of my lord the king who has assigned your food and drink. Why should he see you looking worse than the other young men your age? The king would then have my head because of you.' Daniel then said to the guard whom the chief official had appointed over Daniel, Hannah, Mishael, and Azariah, 'Please test your servants for ten days: Give us nothing but vegetables to eat and water to drink. Then compare our appearance with that of the young men who eat the royal food, and treat treat your servants in accordance with what you see.' So he agreed to this and tested them for ten days. At the end of the ten days they looked healthier and better nourished than any of the young men who ate the royal food. So the guard took away their choice food and the wine that they were to drink and gave them vegetables instead."

(Daniel 1:8-16 NIV)

We know Daniel was participating in a Babylonian training and evaluation program to select the best of the best for the King's service. What wisdom did Daniel demonstrate here? Secondly, what do you believe Daniel would have done had his request been denied?

_____

_____

_____

_____

In your opinion, what factors led Daniel to assert such a health test?

_____

_____

_____

_____

* **Note**: *You may be glad to know that these verses are not a proof test for vegetarianism. See Romans 14:1-4.*

In today's business world, it is not unusual to hear about corporate scandals, embezzlement, and temptations. Although most employers just want honest, hardworking employees, just like Daniel, we may be faced with moral/ethical dilemmas and temptations. As a Christian employee, what is your responsibility to your employer?

_____

_____

_____

_____

Read:

"As a prisoner for the Lord, then, I urge you to live a life worthy of the calling you have received."

(Ephesians 4:1 NIV)

What does this verse teach us?

_____

_____

_____

_____

Chapter 13: Failure to Pray and Pray Correctly

Jesus told the Pharisees that their prayers were terrible, and for that, they hated him. If Jesus had come to earth during our modern times, I wonder if the Pharisees would have accused Jesus of sending them a mean tweet.

I love talking to our Lord through prayer, and I usually pray in short bursts throughout the day whenever something pops into my head. For example, someone might say to me, "I am having trouble with my health. Will you pray for me?" I just do it silently, right at that moment, for two reasons. One, I want to make sure I really do honor my commitment to pray for their need, and second, it is so easy to have an ongoing conversation with our Lord. God's Word says,

"Pray without ceasing."

(I Thessalonians 5:17 KJV)

"Be joyful in hope, be patient in tribulation, constant in prayer."

(Romans 12:2 ESV)

There are other designated times to pray, such as at my weekly prayer meeting group, in conjunction with a religious meeting, a weekly sermon, or a Bible study. Forgive me for saying this, but sometimes I feel like this gets a little weird. Ever been at a service where a guy is called on to pray, and you think that as he begins, he is somehow transported back in time to the 17th century cause you never heard so many thee's and thou's? Then when the guy says Amen, he is magically returned back to present times, and he is speaking normally again. It's a miracle!

Have you ever been in a prayer situation and some guy starts praying, and you were thinking, "We are all going to die here cause this guy will never stop?" You feel like he should be in the U.S. Senate cause he could filibuster for weeks. For sure, I am not the only guy thinking this, but hey, who is ever going to say, "Dude, I rebuke thee cause thou dost pray too long." If God wore a wristwatch, he would be looking at it, and the Holy Spirit would say,

"Hey, please, just quench me now, please, I don't care." Really, I must say, God is not against longer prayers, but it's not the length of your prayer that pleases God. It is not fancy words or 17th-century dialect that impresses God. Please just pray from the heart.

Read:

"And when you pray, do not be like the hypocrites, for they love to pray standing in the synagogues and on the street corners to be seen by others. Truly I tell you they have received their reward in full. But when you pray, go into your room, close the door and pray to your Father, who is unseen. Then your Father, who sees what is done in secret, will reward you. And when you pray, do not keep on babbling like pagans, for they think they will be heard because of their many words. Do not be like them, for your Father knows what you need before you ask him.

(Matthew 6:5-8 NIV)

What directives does God give us for our prayer time, and how to pray? Since God already knows what we need, list some reasons why we should pray.

_____
_____
_____
_____
_____

Read:

"And I will do whatever you ask in my name, so the Father may be glorified in the Son. You may ask me for anything in my name and I will do It."

(John 14:13, 14 NIV)

"But your iniquities have made a separation between you and your God, and your sins have hidden his face so that he does not hear."

(Isaiah 59:2 ESV)

"We know that God does not listen to sinners. He listens to the godly person who does his will."

(John 9:21 NIV)

What gives us the authority to bring our prayer requests to our Father? How does unconfessed sin affect our prayers?

_____

_____

_____

_____

Read:

"Now faith is confidence in what we hope for and assurance about what we do not see."

(Hebrews 11:1 NIV)

"For we live by faith, not by sight."

(II Corinthians 5:7 NIV)

"Have faith in God, Jesus answered."

(Mark 11:22 NIV)

What prerequisite for prayer is found in these verses?

_____

_____

_____

_____

"In him and through faith in him we may approach God with freedom and confidence."

(Ephesians 3:12 NIV)

How does faith affect our prayer life?

_____

_____

_____

_____

"And without faith it is impossible to please God, because anyone who comes to him must believe that he exists and that he rewards those who earnestly seek him."

(Hebrews 11:6 NIV)

In order to receive answers to our prayers, what are the two necessary requirements?

_____

_____

_____

_____

The following verses are all related to prayer. Each verse includes a special promise. Read the verses and list each promise.

James 1:5

_____

_____

_____

Philippians 4:6, 7

_____

_____

_____

Philippians 1:6

_____

_____

_____

Ephesians 3:16

_____

_____

_____

II Corinthians 12:9

_____

_____

_____

The Bible is rich in counsel and truth regarding prayer. Check out these verses:

"Devote yourselves to prayer, being watchful and thankful."

(Colossians 4:2 NIV)

"Call to me and I will answer you and tell you great and unsearchable things you do not know."

(Jeremiah 33:3 NIV)

"Do not be anxious about anything, but in every situation, by prayer and petition, with thanksgiving, present your requests to God."

(Philippians 4:6 NIV)

"In the same way, the Spirit helps us in our weakness. We do not know what to pray for, but the Spirit himself intercedes for us with wordless groans."

(Romans 8:26 NIV)

"Is anyone among you in trouble? Let them pray. Is anyone happy? Let them sing songs of praise. Is anyone among you sick? Let them call the elders of the church, to pray over them, and anoint them with oil in the name of the Lord. And the prayer offered in faith will make the sick person well; the Lord will raise them up. If they have sinned, they will be forgiven. Therefore confess your sins to each other and pray for each other so that you may be healed. The prayer of a righteous person is powerful and effective."

(James 5:13-16 NIV)

"Then will you call upon me and come and pray to me, and I will hear you."

(Jeremiah 29:12 NIV)

"Let us approach God's throne of grace with confidence, so that we may receive mercy and find grace to help us in our time of need."

(Hebrews 4:16 NIV)

"The Lord is far from the wicked, but he hears the prayer of the righteous."

(Proverbs 15:29 NIV)

"I urge then first of all, that petitions, prayers, intercession and thanksgiving be made for all people—for kings and all those in authority, that we may live peaceful and quiet lives in all godliness and holiness."

(I Timothy 2:1,2 NIV)

"This, then, is how you should pray: Our Father in heaven, hallowed be your name, your kingdom come, your will be done, on earth as it is in heaven. Give us today our daily bread. And forgive us our debts, as we also have forgiven our debtors. And lead us not into temptation, but deliver us from the evil one."

(Matthew 6:9-13 NIV)

Prayer is having a conversation with God. Sometimes you may pray long or short prayers. It is always good to praise God for some blessing He has provided to you. Tell God your concerns in a matter of fact address, and mention the needs of others. Close in Jesus's name.

Chapter 14: Wealthy Christian Responsibilities

If you have to wonder if you are in the wealthy class, then you probably are. We know the USA is the world's richest nation. Compared to the world as a whole, today's average American is quite wealthy. Approximately twenty-two million people are millionaires in the USA alone. Almost nine percent of Americans are millionaires, and many more are on the way.

How would you rank your present wealth state? You don't really have to answer. Just think about it.

*Wealthy*_____   *Middle Class*_____   *Poor*_____

Questions about wealth and the Christian's responsibility to the poor are important. What does a wealthy Christian have to do to live a godly life? The Bible does not condemn wealth! It does, however, speak against the love of money.

"The love of money is a root of all kinds of evil. Some people, eager for money, have wandered from the faith and pierced themselves with many griefs."

(I Timothy 6:10 NIV)

There are many Biblical characters that were quite wealthy, and some of them served God very well. Abraham and Job are examples from the early Old Testament. These wealthy individuals served our Lord with distinction. David and certainly Solomon were also quite wealthy. Their relationship with God was bumpy, but money and wealth didn't seem to be at the root of it. In David's case, it was the lust of the flesh and a lack of attention to self-discipline that was his sinful roots. Could David's wealth have been a contributing factor here? The thing about being wealthy is that it can lead to complacency, pride, and independence from God. This is a problem.

Wealth might be evidence of God's blessings. These two verses indicate as much.

"Rich and poor have this in common: The Lord is the maker of them all."

(Proverbs 22:2 NIV)

"Moreover, when God gives someone wealth and possessions, and the ability to enjoy them, to accept their lot and be happy in their toil—this is a gift from God."

(Ecclesiastes 5:19 NIV)

A wealthy person should ask themselves, how did I obtain my wealth? Two other important questions are, how has my wealth changed me, and how will I use my wealth? God's Word is a sober warning to all wealthy individuals. Do not trust in your wealth. You must trust in God!

"For the sun rises with scorching heat and withers the plant; its blossom falls and its beauty is destroyed. In the same way, the rich will fade away even while they go about their business."

(James 1:11 NIV)

"Those who trust in their riches will fall, but the righteous will thrive like a green leaf."

(Proverbs 11:28 NIV)

Back to the first question, a wealthy believer should ask of himself. How did I obtain my wealth? Who cares? God does. Listen to what he says.

"Whoever oppresses a poor man insults his Maker, but he who is generous to the needy honors him."

(Proverbs 14:31 ESV)

"Do not rob the poor, because he is poor, or crush the afflicted at the gate, for the Lord will plead their cause and rob of life those who rob them."

(Proverbs 22:22, 23 ESV)

How you earn your wealth matters to God. I thought of all the ways a person could obtain wealth and, alternatively, why another might become poor. We know some are wealthy through sin, just as some are poor due to sin. Maybe it is a combination of factors influencing one's economic position in life.

How Wealth Was Obtained	Why They Are Poor
Hard work	Sickness/Health Crisis/Mental Issues
Innovation/Initiative/Ideas	Bad decisions/Investments/Law Suits
Inheritance	Crime
Awards/Prizes/Law Suits	Single Parent Households
Athleticism/Talents	Failed Business Ventures
Investments/Insurance	Payouts Government or Other Oppression
Gambling	Terrible Economy
Government Preferential Treatment	War
Marketplace Advantages (Monopolies etc.)	Laziness/Vices
Crime/Cheating	Self-Destruction/Drugs-Alcohol

We can no more assume that the poor live as a result of their own failures or initiatives any more than the wealthy became so through some kind of underhanded scheme. We do know that God has assigned responsibility to Christians to remember the poor.

The final two questions are:

- How has my wealth changed me?

- How will I use my wealth?

The truth is, I don't know the answers to these questions. They are between you and God. My hope and prayer is that you will reflect on these questions before the Lord. What I do know is that God has made a special effort to give you some Biblical counsel. There are two areas of scripture that particularly target this topic.

Biblical Lessons for the Rich Found In I Timothy And Luke

"Command those who are rich in this present world not to be arrogant nor to put their hope in wealth, which is so uncertain, but to put their hope in God, who richly provides us with everything for our enjoyment. Command them to do good, to be rich in good deeds, and to be generous and willing to share. In this way they will lay up treasure for themselves as a firm foundation for the coming age, so that they may take hold of the life that is truly life."

(I Timothy 6:17-19 NIV)

What this verse is saying:

- Don't be arrogant.

- Don't put your hope in wealth.

- Put your hope in God, who provides us with everything for our enjoyment.

- Be rich in good deeds.

- Be generous and willing to share.

- Make investments in eternity.

"Then Jesus said to his host, When you give a luncheon or dinner, do not invite your friends, your brothers or sisters, your relatives, or your rich neighbors; if you do, they may invite you back and so you will be repaid. But when you give a banquet, invite the poor, the crippled, the lame, the blind, and you will be blessed. Although they cannot repay you, you will be repaid at the resurrection of the righteous."

(Luke 14:12-14 NIV)

What this verse is saying:

- Don't be proud.

- Associate with people who are poor and have no power or wealth.

- Do not be conceited.

- Give generously to the needs of others.

- The Lord will honor your gifts with blessings.

In Romans Chapter 12, through the Spirit, Paul writes about spiritual gifts. Read Chapter 12:6-8. Verse 8 says,

"..if it is contributing to the needs of others, let him give generously..."

(Romans 12:6-8 KJV)

Does this verse teach that some have the gift of giving and others do not? What are our basic responsibilities regarding giving?

_____

_____

_____

_____

How do you ensure that your gifts and aid to the poor are used in a positive way? (For example, Say you give money to a homeless person who uses it to purchase alcohol.)

_____

_____

_____

_____

God's desire for us is that we will follow Colossians 3:2.

"Set your minds on things above, not on earthly things."

(Colossians 3:2 NIV)

Read this famous quote from a great author, John Bunyan.

"You have not lived today until you have done something for someone who can never repay you."(5)

- John Bunyan

What are some specific ideas that you could do to love someone who cannot repay you?

_____

_____

_____

_____

Chapter 15: Failure to Speak Out and Get Involved

The Apostles were privileged to witness Jesus speak in person, and they saw His miracles. The Apostles saw Jesus live, die, and then live again. After the resurrection, they spent more time with Him. Jesus gave a command to these men:

> *"Therefore go and make disciples of all the nations, ...teaching them to obey everything I have commanded you. I am with you always, to the very end of the age."*

(Matthew 28:19, 20 NIV)

Jesus further instructed His disciples, saying,

> *"But you will receive power when the Holy Spirit comes on you: and you will be witnesses in Jerusalem, and in all Judaea and Samaria, and to the ends of the earth."*

(Acts 1:8 NIV)

All believers today share this command from God, known as "The Great Commission." Just like the Apostles, we are to tell the world the Good News of Jesus Christ, oftentimes, to people who really don't want to hear it. No believer should be surprised that the world would rather that Christians remain silent. Satan, the father of lies, is successfully working to mislead, manipulate, and distort the truth in this present world. In the end, we know he is a loser, but for now, it can get discouraging. Consider that over sixty million lives have already been sacrificed through abortion. Today any formal mention of God has been removed from our public schools. Prayer and the ten commandments are forbidden in the classroom. Our religious liberties are under attack for nothing more than speaking the truth of God's word.

We should consider the Apostle's response in Acts 5. The silencers at this time in history are really no different than today. Cancel culture is not a new concept. After Jesus challenged His Apostles, he ascended to heaven. His Apostles were trained and fully equipped to follow God's will, and they did. They preached and taught Jesus Christ in and around Jerusalem. There was nothing that would keep them from doing this. Then the Apostles were brought before the council of the high priest. These same proud, religious leaders were responsible for false accusations and plotting against our Lord.

Here is what happened as told in Acts 5.

"The Apostles were brought in and made to appear before the Sanhedrin to be questioned by the high priest. 'We gave you strict orders not to teach in this name,' he said. 'Yet you have filled Jerusalem with your teaching and are determined to make us guilty of this man's blood.' Peter and the other Apostles replied, 'We must obey God rather than human beings! The God of our ancestors raised Jesus from the dead—whom you killed by hanging him on a cross. God exalted him to his own right hand as Prince and Savior that he might bring Israel to repentance and forgive their sins. We are witnesses of these things, and so is the Holy Spirit, whom God has given to those who obey him.' When they (the religious leaders) heard this they were furious and wanted to put them to death."

(Acts 5:27-33 NIV)

These ungodly religious men had the Apostles beaten and then let go, commanding them again that they should not speak in the name of Jesus. What was the Apostle's reaction to all this? They went away and rejoiced that they were counted worthy to suffer for Jesus's name, and they did not cease to preach and teach the message of salvation through Jesus Christ.

If you and I believe what we say we do, then we also must preach and teach Jesus. Consider the illustration below.

Jesus, During the Time with His Apostles	Jesus, Today During Your Time
Apostles and believers followed Him	Christian believers follow Him
Jesus preached and taught	His word endures in scripture
Jesus performed miracles	Today Jesus performs miracles
Jesus saved souls	Today Jesus saves souls

Jesus was opposed	Today Jesus is opposed
Jesus commanded the Apostles	Today Jesus commands
to preach and teach	Christians to preach and teach

"Jesus Christ is the same yesterday and today and forever."

(Hebrews 13:8 NIV)

Despite everything written in this chapter thus far, a Christian purpose is not solely limited to just winning souls. The diversity of spiritual gifts and the many duties we perform require a believer to focus on a variety of responsibilities. A good man named Tom Minnery wrote a book several years ago titled "Why You Can't Stay Silent." I am going to share a paragraph he wrote which is just as relevant today as when he first authored his book.

He writes,

*"Our Constitution preamble begins with, "We the People."
Christian people, as much as anyone else, constitute "The
People." We have as much right to contend for our views, as does
any other citizen. And if we sit idly by while the wicked rule
without doing what we can to change matters, then we, ultimately
are to blame." (6)*

Today more than I can ever remember, there is an open battle for the minds of our youth. There is an unabashed open assault in an effort to teach a liberal unholy philosophy. Consider what we hear regularly happening in our schools while Godly parents try to keep the focus on basic education. Parents across America are wise to the indoctrination that has been and is taking place in our public schools. Consider some of these latest challenges:

- **Critical Race Theory** - Teaches systematic racism and identifies privileged and oppressed classes fostering racial divisions.

119

- **The 1619 Project** - Portrays America as a Fundamentally Racist Nation and makes slavery the central story of American History.

- **Gender Identity** - Some programs encourage young students to consider identifying as the opposite sex by example.

- **Sexually Explicit Materials** - Some Library materials are too graphic for young minds and promote an agenda.

- **Over-Reaching Heath Mandates** - Teachers Union memos have targeted public policy regardless of scientific findings.

With all this liberal social engineering going on, who knows when there is any time to teach elementary, middle, and high school basic core curriculums?

School Board members have important responsibilities, including choosing textbooks and curriculums along with allocating financial resources. It is more important for today's parents to find out each School Board candidate's positions when deciding for whom to vote. Parents in Loudoun County, Virginia, to Southlake, Texas, have already been energized. We need this effort in every school district across America. Some states are working to make changes allowing tax dollars to follow each student. Maine is one state that has already taken such action. This would allow parents to better afford private schools as an alternative to the many failing or misguided public schools.

Is it OK for Christians to have strong opinions on taxes, marriage, abortion, and other government policies? What do you think?

_____

_____

_____

_____

_____

There are numerous Bible verses related to these matters. Here are just a few I picked out. Read each verse.

- **Obeying Government** - There is no power given except by God. Romans 3:1-7

- **Marriage** - Is between a man and a woman. Genesis 2:24; Matthew 19;4,5; Ephesians 5:31

- **Abortion** - Genesis 9:6; Job 10:8; Psalms 22:9,10

- **Taxes** - Jesus paid the Temple tax so as not to cause an offense. Matthew 17:24-27

- **Taxes** - Render unto Caesar. Luke 20: 19-26

Paul recognized his Roman citizenship. As a citizen, it was the Roman government that gave Paul the right to a trial before any judgements or punishments were levied against him. Paul's rights were about to be violated when he was to be beaten without due process. Paul pointed this out to the Roman centurion in Acts Chapter 22.

"As they stretched him out to flog him, Paul said to the centurion standing there, 'Is it legal for you to flog a Roman citizen who hasn't even been found guilty?' When the centurion heard this, he went to the commander and reported it. 'What are you going to do?' He asked. 'This man is a Roman citizen.' The commander went to Paul and asked. 'Tell me, are you a Roman citizen.' 'Yes I am,' he answered. Then the commander said, 'I had to pay a lot of money for my citizenship.' 'But I was born a citizen,' Paul replied. Those who were about to interrogate him withdrew immediately. The commander himself was alarmed when he realized that he had put Paul, a Roman citizen, in chains."

(Acts 22:25-.29 NIV)

The United States Constitution grants every American citizen the right to have religious freedom. If a Christian's religious freedom is denied, then that same American citizen may seek relief in the courts. This year a football coach named Coach Kennedy filed a lawsuit alleging that his religious freedom was being denied. His school district had refused to grant him the freedom to pray after high school football games. The U.S. Supreme Court decided in Coach Kennedy's favor.

What concerns me most today is the battle for the hearts and minds of our children. The liberals say they want inclusion. Just make sure you don't include any mention of God. Liberals want to teach their version of history, which of course, leaves out the most cataclysmic event that ever happened in the history of the world, the great flood. Liberals want to teach science but fail to mention how it is God that formed Adam and Eve as male and female in His likeness and created the vast universe. Liberals want to talk about philosophy but attempt to suppress all discussion of the greatest philosopher that ever lived and lives today, Jesus Christ. School Districts need to know that they cannot lawfully deny the freedom of religion. Today more parents are opting for homeschooling, charter schools, and private Christian schools than ever before. We can understand why.

In like manner, local governments must know and understand they cannot discriminate against churches in planning and zoning decisions. Sometimes local governments don't want to approve a church construction project. True reasons for these actions are usually masked. These reasons seem to be varied, ranging from discrimination to simply not liking the church's tax exemption status. My Christian attorney friends have duly noted that some local governments have purposefully or unknowingly written unconstitutional zoning and planning laws or unfairly asserted eminent domain privileges. Like Paul, Christians should be willing to challenge these unlawful actions. There are two outstanding organizations that are standing in the gap, willing to help Christians whose religious liberties have been abused or denied by employers or government entities. These are the American Center for Law and Justice and the Liberty Council. Another great organization, the Heritage Foundation, has provided Christian lawmakers with guidance in legislative initiatives in an effort to protect our religious freedoms. Your support and involvement in these organizations would be welcomed.

As Christians, we remember we are not to be bound to this world, and our citizenship is in Heaven. But like Paul, we must take on the mantle of the high calling of God in Jesus Christ. Philippians Chapter 3 warns us that "many live as enemies of the cross of Christ." Clearly, we see this, and we are aware that we must speak out and get involved.

What do/will you do to speak out and get involved?

_____

_____

_____

_____

Conclusion

It would be easy for an author to write an accusatory book about sin. There is a vast target audience for such a literary work. After reading this book, hopefully, you don't feel this book's purpose is to tear you down. When an unbeliever first hears the gospel message and really contemplates it, there is a time of introspection. The unbeliever looks inward and admittedly says, "Yes, I am a sinner, and I am lost. Yes, I need Christ to be my Lord and Savior". As you continue to be transformed, my hope for this book is that you, as a Christian, will look inward and be introspective concerning accepted sins.

Every time we talk with someone, read a book or listen to a speaker, we change. Change is good, but change can be hard. We have a sinful nature, and believers must strive to pattern our lives after Christ. We need to change and put off our old nature and put on the new. God's presence requires us to change. At least we are not shooting at a moving target. We like some stability, and we are comforted by God's unchanging character.

Consider these verses:

"He who is the Glory of Israel does not lie or change his mind; for he is not a human being, that he should change his mind."

(I Samuel 15:29 NIV)

Another verse in James says,

> *"...the Father of the Heavenly lights, who does not change like shifting shadows."*

(James 1:17 NIV)

Ultimately, each of us as individuals is responsible for how we live our lives and for making the necessary changes. You are not responsible for me, and likewise, I am not responsible for you. We all must individually strive to be changed to be in His image.

How has this book changed you?

_____

_____

_____

_____

On the day that Jesus had healed the blind man in John Chapter 9, on two occasions, this now formerly blind man was hauled before the local religious leaders for trial. The religious leaders were furious and upset that this Jesus would have miraculous power over blindness. They determined to have a trial and get to the bottom of this outrage. Of all the nerve, what kind of sinner would heal a blind man? The problem was they were terrible courtroom lawyers, but they tried. First, they brought in witnesses, the parents, to verify that the healed man was really their son and also to confirm that their son had indeed been born blind. Oh man, that didn't help cause the parents said, "yep, that's our boy, and yep, he was born blind." Now I wasn't there, but I have to wonder if Peter was in the back of the synagogue, holding his hand over his mouth to keep from laughing out loud. Then, the not so wise religious leaders said, "no need to call in the many people that actually witnessed the miracle." Good thing these guys did not have to go up against Perry Mason, right?

During the second trial, with the formerly blind man, the religious leaders once again asked the exact same questions, "What did Jesus do to you, and how did he open your eyes?" Now Perry Mason would have immediately objected here and said, "Objection! They

125

are badgering the witness." Now here is where the religious leaders were looking bad, so, to save face, they said, "Hey dude, we follow Moses, but we don't even know where your guy Jesus is from." Finally, they unknowingly spoke the truth. Moses brought the law, and the law kills, but Jesus brought saving grace. The religious leaders chose to proudly follow the path of condemnation instead of taking the free gift of salvation.

Now, this is a very critical point in the trial. The formerly blind man really lets them have it with a full cannon of truth. Right after the man heard them admit that they had no idea where Jesus had come from, he said,

> *"..Now that is remarkable! You don't know where he comes from, yet he opened my eyes. We know that God does not listen to sinners. He listens to the godly person who does his will. Nobody has ever heard of opening the eyes of a man born blind. If this man (Jesus) were not from God, he could do nothing."*

(John 9:30-33)

Later knowing that the healed blind man had been thrown out of the synagogue, Jesus met with him. The blind man finally recognized Jesus for who he was, the Savior, and he immediately professed his faith and worshiped him. Then Jesus said,

> *"For judgement I have come into this world, so that the blind will see and those who see will become blind."*

(John 9:39 NIV)

The religious leaders, standing nearby, asked Jesus if he was saying they were blind. Here is his response. Jesus said unto them,

> *"If ye were blind, ye should have no sin: but now ye say, We see; therefore your sin remains."*

126

Like all believers, the religious leader's prideful condition would not allow them to admit their own sins. Sin separates us from God! Even after becoming a believer, sin can hamper our relationship with God. Lord, help us not to be blind to any sin in our lives. Let us strive to honor our Lord by defeating "Our Accepted Sins."

Remember the words of David from Psalm 66,

> *"If I had cherished iniquity in my heart, the Lord would not have listened." May God bless you in these endeavors!*

Notes

1. _Healthline.com_ Obesity - Moores, Danielle - Updated
    7/31/20

2. Wiersbe, Warren Real Worship, Battle Ground or Holy
    Ground p. 32

3. Wiersbe, Warren Sermon Notes. Covington, Ky. Calvary
    Baptist Church. Date Unknown

4. Henry, Matthew The NIV Matthew Henry Commentary on
    the Bible (Concise) I Cortinthians 10:23-33 - Harper
    Collins

5. Bunyan, John The Poetry of John Bunyan - Volume II
    amazon.sg 1/26/17

6. Minnery, Tom Why You Can't Stay Silent - Tyndall House
    Publishers, Weaton, Illinois 2001

Acknowledgements

Iron Sharpens Iron

This book wouldn't have been possible without the encouragement of my friends, family, or my publishing company and editorial team, Amazon Pro Hub. Thank you for everything you guys have done for my book.

The following individuals (listed in no particular order) have had an influence on my spiritual walk. Some have only been a part of my life for a short term, and there are a couple of persons on this list that I have never met personally, but nonetheless, I have benefited from their work and ministry. Some were teachers, encouragers, and others were wonderful examples to me on how to be a better Christian. Some I knew well and others I hardly knew, but I was inspired by their character.

Dr. Warren Wiersbe	Bob & Glena White	Joe & Donna Griffin
Cedric Witcomb	Jim & Geri Roads	Pastor Galen & Jeanette Call
Roy & Barbara Davoll	Richard & Pam Peace	Pastor Randy Faulkner
Willard & Joyce Slade	Tom & Janice Kerr	Pastor Bruce Peters
Bill & Ruth Carroll	Gerry & Kim Tucker	Charlie & Laurie Walton

Steve Kelly	Dan Rothfuss	Pat & Turtle Bradford
Ed Meece	Diane Gates	Jim Stow
Don Sieber	Mary Sefzik	David Baker
Gary Bricking	Pastor Robert Jeffress	Sarah Huckabee Sanders
Mrs. D. B. Eastep	Mike Farrell	John & Ruby Heisler
Jack Ruffley	Steve & Bobbi Freeburne	Jim Coleman
Stan & Linda Riches	Ron & Karen Sollberger	Rick Warken
C.S. Lewis	Pastor John MacArthur	Dr. James Dobson
Dale & Becky Armstrong	Bob Vallandingham	Wayne Bridges
Dan Eastep	Jerry & Kristy Thornton	Pastor David Graham
Dave Steele	Bob Ledford	Bob & Kathy Tidrow
Jim Stanley	Billy Graham	Franklin Graham
Paul Wilson	Guy King	Omer Mastin
Bob McConnell	Charlie Bush	Barry True
Frank & Gail Venturino	Coleen Hannika	Bob Walsh
Daniel & Amy Chilton	Kevin & Courtney Black	Helen Peeno
Kerby Anderson	Jim & Sylvia Tereschuk	Marc & Rhonda Leediker
Barbara Black	Jimmy Taulbee	Van & Wilma Needham
Bob Kopich	Rodney Eldridge	John Christopher
Stan Caudell	Sharon Norberg	Galen & Debbie Bridges

Marlene Hamilton	Phil Taylor	Rebecca Burnett-Grubb
Jeff & Susan Starnes	Dick Murgatroyd	Scott & Jean Kimmich
Mark & Linda Gray	Jack & Kelly Westwood	Mike & Peggy Parker
Jim & Donna Tarkington	Gerri Dyson	Larry & Paula Bussard
Karol King	Myron & Kathy Wolfe	Jennifer Brown Gentile
Pastor Jim Rosner	Cheryl Kopp	Bob & Debbie Yoxthimer
Tom & Emma Brumback	David Barnett	Doug & Betsy Peeno
Bill & Shirley Peeno	Carl & Pam Girdler	Clarence & Bonnie Peeno
Paul & Judy Kaiser	Holli Chilton	Brent Brewster
Sam & Flora Black	Thelma Collins	Kevin & Linda Marksberry
Mike & Pat Black	Tom Crouch	

About the Author

Keith presently lives near Dallas with his wife, Barbara. They were married in 1975 in Kentucky. He enjoys golfing and spending time with eight grandkids when he is not busy writing. After leaving a corporate business career, he went into teaching for a few years and then back to business and writing. Keith has been active in Christian ministries and was a founding church member. They presently attend First Baptist of Dallas. Keith is already working on his next book, and the title will be announced soon.

Keith has worked in the following **Christian Ministries**:

- Deacon and Elder in two separate churches

- Adult and Youth Bible Teacher

- Christian School Board Member

- Teacher Dave Ramsey and Ron Blue Financial Programs

- Salvation Army Board-Member

- Family First Political Action Committee (PAC) Board Member

Keith has played his part in several **community activities,** including the following:

- Newport Optimists Club, Past President

- United Way Regional Board Member

- Led and served in numerous fundraising initiatives

- Transit Authority Board of Directors (TANK)

- Served on Regional and State Chamber of Commerce Boards

Keith's accomplishments include 50-plus years of business experience. His services include the following:

- **General Manager** - Fortune 500 Company

- **President & CEO**, Black Management Services, LLC

- **Member of Board of Directors**, Boone National Bank

- **State Chairman** - American Legislative Exchange Council

Keith's **educational history** is as follows:

- MBA from Northern Ky. University

- Attended Darden Executive Management School of Business - University of Virginia.